What **YOU** *Are* **THINKING?**

What *Are* YOU THINKING?

AN ADVENTURE IN THINKING WONDERLAND

Basil G.Phillips

SPM

What Are You Thinking ?
by Basil G. Phillips

Copyright © 2011 by Basil G. Phillips

First edition 2015
ISBN: 9781613796931

Scripture quotations unless otherwise marked are taken from the Holy Bible, *NIV,*® *New International Version*®. Copyright ©1973,1978,1984, 2010 by Biblica, Inc.™ Used by permission. All rights reserved.

Scripture quotations marked *KJV* are from the *King James Version* of the Bible.

Published by
Special Project Ministries (A Ministry of OM International)
P.O. Box 660
Forest Hill, London SE 23 3ST
United Kingdom

Printed and bound in India by
Authentic Media, Secunderabad 500 067, Telangana, India.
e-mail: printing@ombooks.org

Dedication

I dedicate this book, first to the Glory of God which is the primary motive for the initiative. Next, to the loving and never-fading memory of my late beloved wife, Phyllis and to

my precious daughter, Patti.

CONTENTS

ACKNOWLEDGEMENTS

Without hesitation I say thanks to my cousin Arthur Phillips Sr., who for many years kept reminding me to write a book! To him will be delivered the first printed copy. Thanks to Ms. Carol Williamson of the Galilee Gospel Chapel church staff, who diligently worked through my hand-written scribbles to produce "clean" print-ready copies of the manuscript.

Special thanks to Sir Maxwell Pennycooke, my Canadian friend, whose comments I invited from the early stages of the first rough draft! Sir Maxwell deserves much praise for his detailed scrutiny and very kind encouragements. Thanks also to the kind souls whose comments I sought in an early release of the rough draft of the first section. Thanks for their enthusiastic comments. These are: Dr. David Epstein Sr. Pastor of Calvary Baptist Church N.Y.; George Verwer Founder of Operation Mobilization; Dale

Rhoton Co-founder of Operation Mobilization; Dr. Roger Willmore Keswick conference speaker; Bill Welte CEO America's Keswick and Dr. Keith Phillips Fellow Pastor at the Galilee Gospel Chapel N.Y. To my daughter Patti for her various "helping hands." My sincere thanks to all!

PREFACE

Emily Dickinson once wrote "There is no frigate like a book to take us lands away, nor any course like a page of prancing poetry." I would add, there is nothing like a friendly, exciting, enjoyable, and insightful conversation strolling through **THINKING WONDERLAND.**

Welcome to a stimulating reading experience. My greetings to those of you who over many years have been interacting with me in my role as Corporate Executive; Pastor, Entrepreneur, Visiting Professor, Public Speaker, Personal Friend and Family Member, and especially my cousin, Arthur Phillips, Sr., who never ceased to remind me to write a book. I have been repeatedly asked to write an autobiography. Sorry to disappoint you, but I hope you will not regret the choice I made to invite my reader to stroll with me in a dialogue exchange as we enjoy the serenity of an imaginary **THINKING WONDERLAND.**

If you haven't asked this question – perhaps you should. Why another book on any subject or topic. It used to be the local library or bookstore where you would find any book to suit your reading fancy or taste. Now thanks to our Age of Aquarius in technology, we can Google (or other search engine) any topic and get linked into unlimited information sources.

Everything imaginable is out there on the Internet. Everyone is writing, Blogging, Tweeting, you name it! So again, why this book? Let me tell you up front in a few sincere words. I have an irrepressible urge to share my thoughts as I observed things and people in my universe about and around me. Also, I am urged to share what I have experienced by God's grace, in the vicissitudes of a nearly miraculous life. My expectation is to have an unusual conversation about Thinking with my reader.

Now, it's just the two of us strolling through this imaginary **Thinking Wonderland.** We will be thinking about the wonder of God, Thinking about the mystery of man and finally about the possibility of a personal relationship with an **Omnipotent, Omniscient and Omnipresent God.**

Our dialogue will be informative, invigorating, inspiring, and insightful and I hope enjoyable. The introduction on the next page will escort you to the first step on our unhurried journey through **THINKING WONDERLAND.** By the way, it's all about "What are You Thinking?" or even better, what can we think together.

INTRODUCTION
WHAT ARE YOU THINKING?

Many centuries ago in the heyday of the mighty Greek empire there lived in Athens a famous wise man (philosopher) whose name was Socrates. Someone asked him: "How would he describe himself?" His reply – "A midwife." He explained that he observed young men (his students) who were pregnant with thoughts but were unable to give birth. My role, he said, as midwife, is to help them deliver their **thinking.**

The civilization that we enjoy today with all the benefits of science, technology, social ethics, etc., owes huge debts of gratitude to Socrates and the thinkers of his genre. Your ability and mine to think are a direct result of that mysterious phenomenon between our ears called the human brain – or better stated – the think factory. Our brain is the indispensable source of our thinking and is at the core of all our thoughts. The ability to think was not reserved for the ancient intelligence of our ancestors. That unique ability was transferred in the DNA of every person in our species. Is this an amazing thought or what?

Here is another amazing fact! About five hundred years after the Greek era of Socrates, et al, there lived in Israel a man who, like Socrates, spent much of his time in the streets of Galilee and Judea in the company of his students – called disciples – and among huge crowds that followed him to hear his inspiring words and to witness his miraculous works. This man announced himself to be the Son of God as well as God the Son. Unlike Socrates, he proved beyond the deepest doubts, by his miracles and his message that he could do anything. He explicitly stated that for him nothing was impossible. In other words, his power was so infinite that everything was imaginable and possible. He also claimed to know everything, and could be everywhere at any time.

This Jewish man was, by the way, a man called Jesus of Nazareth and later referred to by his followers as the Lord Jesus Christ. Repeated references will be made to this revered extraordinary man from Nazareth of Galilee (Israel) whose supernatural attributes evoked words like these: "Never did any man speak like this man"; "He speaks with absolute authority and not like our teachers." This God – man repeatedly raised a timeless question: **What are you thinking?** Jesus, in the course of his numerous dialogues, sermons, seminars, and social exchanges, repeatedly asked his audience what were they thinking. He wanted to catch their attention on this very important subject of **thinking.**

Our Lord wanted to broaden the perspective of his listeners and followers on the landscape of thinking. For example; he saw many shepherds caring for sheep so deeply that they would risk life and limb to rescue one lost sheep. What were they thinking of that shepherd and his poor and lost sheep. Was it the commercial value of one sheep or the spectacular compassion of the shepherd? Jesus wanted them to ask themselves what were they thinking about the predicament of that one sheep, who wandered away and hopelessly went astray. What did they think about the choice of leaving the ninety-nine sheep in the care of other shepherds while risking his own life in a precarious search and rescue adventure to find his lone, poor, helpless, and nearly hopeless sheep.

In another example, our Lord switched from the heartrending parable of the lost sheep with its emotional and ceremonial overtones to the heartwarming illustration of a father's love for his wayward younger son. This story is a Bible classic known as the Parable of the Prodigal Son. As in the case of the Shepherd and his wandering and lost sheep, the thinking focus in this parable was about a loving Father and a lost and wandering son.

This younger son (family of four) left home with his pockets bulging with inheritance money and his heart set on having the time of his life. In a short while, the story says, his good times and his inherited money went south while he drifted, aimlessly as an illegal immigrant in a foreign land. He finally found work caring for pigs.

The highlight of this young man's profligate experience was that – He started to Think Straight! He thought of his father, his home, his family and their servants and then he composed a reentry script dripping with humility, remorse and contrition. He, in fact, put his thinking into words like these: "I will arise and return to my father, and say to him, I have sinned against heaven and before you. I am no more worthy to be called your son. Make me one of your hired servants." Wow! Some straight thinking, kicked in, didn't it? The story says that his loving and compassionate father received him joyfully into his waiting arms, and dressed him up and had a great reception party to celebrate his wayward son's return. Choking with joyful emotion, this legendary loving father said: "This my son was lost and is found, was dead but now is alive again." What a story! No wonder this Biblical parable is known worldwide both to young and old in the course of over two thousand years since it was first told.

This book is not a sermon about the philosophy of thinking but a sincere attempt to stimulate and emphasize the importance of what and how we think.

You picked up this book because you, my thinking partner, are endowed by our Creator with the apparatus for **thinking** – far – far beyond what you ever thought you could think.

My prayer is that this brief dialogue, exposition, conversation, or exchange on thinking will allow me, like Socrates, or better yet, like our Lord Jesus, to assist you in giving birth to thought that you have never thought before and that those thoughts may lead you to places you have never been before.

We will talk about people before our time and how they thought about God, and how we think about God in our worldview today. We will talk about "Man" and how men thought about other men, then we will talk about ourselves (my fellow traveler and me) and how/what we think about our relationship with God. You may be thinking – is that even remotely possible – a relationship with God? We will get to that later on toward the end of our dialogue.

Finally, a brief epilogue will give some insight into the author's life and what influenced his thinking. Please promise to continue reading thoughtfully, promise to stay with me as we stroll through the amazing wonderland of thinking.

I promise you that you will not regret this unusually stimulating experience. Trust me, if you hang in, when we reach the end of our journey, you will want to keep going. So, let's get started.

PART I

WHAT ARE YOU THINKING ABOUT GOD?

THE WONDER OF OUR UNIVERSE

CHAPTER I

DISCOVER YOUR GIFT OF THINKING

Did you know you are a gifted thinker?

Did I catch you off guard? In other words, did I catch you not thinking? Well to be sure there is not a waking moment when we are not **Thinking! Thinking! Thinking!** Actually, this distinctive human capability of thinking is exceptional and sets us apart from all other species on planet earth. May I now have the pleasure of your company as we take a one-step, two-step, three-step excursion into this fascinating wonderland of THINKING? Since you have agreed to come with me I'll tell you where we are going and I am sure you will be engaged, interested and stay connected. Please take no exception or offence to my verbal habit in referring to you as "Friend."

As we start this exciting adventure into **Thinking Wonderland,** here is a relaxing warm-up exercise. First, did you know that you can't think without words? No matter what language you speak, if you think you can think without words – take a minute and give it a serious try. How did you do? That, my friend, is the uniqueness of the human mind/ brain. That, my friend is a **God-given gift** to each of us. With the words that we have learned in our early years we form thoughts i.e. we ask questions, contrive answers, we reason, develop ideas, imagine the possible and dream the impossible, we conceive good and evil. In short with words we **Think.**

Bible stories of the ancient people groups and other historical records help us understand how this mysterious thinking apparatus works. For example, in one of the Bible Psalms (Ps. 8:3) David a legendary King of Israel is caught gazing upward into the vast expanse of the mideastern starlit skies – here are his expressions of awe: "When I think of the heavens, the work of thy fingers, the moon, the stars, which you have ordained what is man that you think about him." Another time, King David observed the rising sun at the early dawn and traced its trajectory toward its western setting as the twilight made room for the darkness of night. David was asking this profound question: what is man that you made him with such a mind/brain with capacity to admire and be astonished at the mystery and majesty of the cosmic creation? Man is a **Thinker!**

Oh, what a beautiful journey we are starting. Let's not rush this beautiful experience. Let's go step by step or we will miss some very important things that you perhaps have not thought of before. For example, in our post-modern secular culture, there are at least two popular sacred cows, i.e., things people don't easily share with others – their politics and their religion – who they vote for and what they believe in – or what they think about God.

When you agreed to start this trip with me, if you recall, I mentioned that one of the stops we would make as we entered this wonderland of thinking was – **Thinking about God.** In other words, my friendly question to you is: **What are you Thinking About God?** While you are thinking up a friendly answer, let me share with you a few of my thoughts. We have just recalled the emotional outbursts of King David's thoughts (Ps. 8:3). He was not an astronomer or a cosmologist. He was just a lowly Jewish shepherd boy turned King. How did he get so connected with the wonder and beauty of the starlit heavens at night and the majesty of the rising sun at early dawn, and the fascinating drama of the setting sun as it dipped below the twilight horizon? Well, there is a verse in the good book – The Bible – It says that **"There is a spirit in man: and the inspiration of the Almighty giveth them understanding." (Job 32:8) So here is a provocative thought:**

God surrounds all of us with compelling and convincing evidence of Himself in the wonder and splendor of His marvelous universe. So like David, I am mesmerized when gazing upward into the mystery of space and seeing the display of the creative genius of a God who has ultimate intelligence and incredible power and who is also invisible to our eyes. There is a verse in the Bible (Rom. 1:20) that is the origin of my thoughts. It says: "God has from, the dawn of time, put into the heart (mind) of man (all human beings) the instinct to recognize that the invisible God is the creator of the universe. This God remains a mystery and man is forever trying to discover – **who is this God?"**

It is this instinct that triggers my thinking about God. Did I always share this view of God? Not really! Let's stay on point about your thinking about God. The point is, I came around to thinking about God because admittedly, I felt so very vulnerable. I saw people going through the ups and downs of life and then I observed their mortality – in other words I saw that many people of all ages, the rich and the poor, the ignorant and the intelligent, the good people and the bad people – they all at some time inevitably surrendered to death. I wondered, like the Bible character Job who asked the question – "If a man dies shall he live again?" I had no answer. But I kept thinking about the mystery of God! As I kept thinking about God, I realized that my quiet and private curiosity was not of my own prompting. Remember the fact I mentioned earlier, that God has placed in the mind of every human being the instinct to be connected with someone beyond himself? Let's keep this in mind. Also, let's keep an open mind. We may discover that even by the most rigorous analysis of things far and near, things seen and unseen – there must be some reason why we human beings, think the way we do. We not only think, but raise questions to think about. Even more amazing is the fact that despite the obstacles that threaten the survival of our ancestors and our current generation, we have been able to think of ways to conquer and not be conquered, to overcome and not be overcome. In other words our civilization survives because we are thinking.

Isn't it exciting to think that we can continue this adventure into **wonderland of thinking** by celebrating a fact that we may not even realize? That fact, my friend, is that we are uniquely gifted with the ability to think in ways that no other creature or species on our planet can. So, what do you think about that? Are you all psyched up? Let's go for it!

CHAPTER 2

A PEEK AT THE BIG THREE O'S

No one on planet Earth has this resume

Somewhere I heard some religious talk about **omnipotence, omniscience** and **omnipresence.** My thinking lead me further down the path of curiosity. What is the meaning of these attributes of God? These three attributes belong only to God. No man can fit these descriptions or can be worthy of these attributes. I reasoned that God alone has these unique supernatural and extraordinary attributes (qualities). What do they mean and where can I find out more about this Mysterious God? My instincts continued to whisper **Keep Thinking! Keep Thinking!** A light flashed – Ah-Ah! Information source is what I needed to find! At this point let's pause for a bit of reflection. Once in a while, ever recall some sound bite, some wise saying, some catchy saying that sticks in your mind? Here is one that I heard or read some place – or better yet – I may have made it up in a philosophical moment. Here it is! **Information IS WHERE YOU FIND IT!**

Keep in mind that on this curiosity path during our journey into **Thinking Wonderland** together we will be inspired by the truism of that sound-bite **Information IS WHERE YOU FIND IT!** So, where do I find this information that enables thinking about this God uniquely described as **Omnipotent, Omniscient** and **Omnipresent?** So where do you think I found a trove of information? In Greek philosophy, in the writings of the age of enlightenment thinkers, the works of celebrated world-class scientists, the archives of metaphysics et al? Fact is that I did take a peek through some of these windows of information called secular knowledge but can you ever guess where I found the most valuable information that formed the basis for all my thinking about God and about everything thinkable? Are you ready with your best guess? Let me tell you with all the passion that human expression makes possible – I found the source of information to facilitate my thinking about God in the sacred pages of a book you may or may not have heard about – It is the indisputable best seller of all time – **THE HOLY BIBLE!**

Incidentally, I brought along a copy of the Bible in my tote bag for our convenient reference. If you take no exception I can share some references with you as we stroll along together through **Thinking Wonderland.**

If you recall, I mentioned the big **Three Os** – **O**mnipotence, **O**mniscience and **O**mnipresence. You must be thinking – are those the only three attributes of the God you are inviting me to think about? As a matter of fact, they are not by a long shot. This is just an appetizer for our thoughts. Other attributes of God are Holiness, Love, Grace, Mercy, Kindness, Patience, etc. These, by His design, have been integrated into our human experience while the big **Three Os** are inexpressibly beyond our human scope, capacity and capability. That's why any respectable dictionary will describe those three (3) attributes as only belonging to **God and God alone!** Is that amazing or what? You might be saying – I did not know that. Well, you are in the company of so many others who do not have this information. Do you get the feeling that the journey we started into **Thinking Wonderland** is going to be an unforgettable trek and it will get more exciting with each passing moment. I have to confess that I am full of what you may call spiritual excitement and perhaps even a touch of animation.

Let me share some insights into my thinking about God. Remember that our key source of information is the Holy Bible. Where better to start reaching for this information but in the first book (GENESIS) and the very first verse of the first chapter? One word of warning: This chapter and this particular verse has been a lightening rod of scientific, philosophic and religious contention and conversation for ages. You may have heard of men like Voltaire, Friedrich Nietzsche, Thomas Paine, Bertrand Russell, Carl Sagan and recently Richard Dawkins and not to leave out the female thought warriors like Madeline O'Hare and Susan Jacoby, president of Free Thinkers, USA. The list goes on to include a variety of published opinions, speculations and **Thinking About God.**

Well, let's manage our thoughts as we move along so we don't get distracted. What does the Bible say by way of information about the Omnipotence of God – The first of the big **Three Os?** Genesis chapter 1 verse 1 says: <u>**"In the Beginning God Created The Heavens and the Earth."**</u> You will notice that the opening verse does not say that in the beginning there was a <u>**Big Bang!**</u> Incidentally, the Bible does say that the universe will end in a <u>**Big Bang**</u> and a colossal cosmic meltdown. Did you know that? This information is clearly stated in the New Testament passage (2 Peter 3:10) that says "But the day of the Lord will come as a thief in the night, in which the heavens shall pass away with a great noise (Big Bang) and the elements shall melt with fervent heat, the earth also and the works that are therein shall be burned up."

So there we go! The Bible makes it indisputably clear that the Omnipotent God began the beginning of all beginnings with His spoken word and not a big bang – The big bang will come at the end of time! Before we start thinking about this Omnipotent God we will need a very important ingredient – Faith. Have you heard of Faith? Sounds like a tease question doesn't it?

CHAPTER 3

THE FAITH FACTOR

Every day we practice faith

Faith is so much a part of our everyday life that we sometimes don't think much about it. For example, how many times have you climbed aboard a commercial airplane and taken an assigned seat without a thought about the competence of the pilots? Was this their first flight at the controls? Are they sober and able to fly this bird safely to your destination? Your faith says: not to worry – the pilots must be experienced and checked out to fly this plane or they wouldn't be in the cockpit. That, my friend is faith in action! Here is another interesting example of faith. Every single moment we breathe the life sustaining air that we can never see, we are not about to question if it's safe to breathe because its toxicity can kill us. If we did, we would all be calling for gas masks. Why aren't we concerned about the lethal effect of breathing the air that floats in and out of our nostrils? Could this be **because of our Faith** in our government?

We believe that if the air we breathe to stay alive were lethal, our government would not only warn us but provide means for our survival. We also believe that there is an agency of government that monitors the air quality on a 24/7 schedule and that there is an alert warning system should there be an air contaminant threat. The truth be told, my dear friend, should there be such an air contamination threat, there would not be enough gas masks to save a small fraction of the national population. Despite this reality, we keep on breathing because our Faith relieves us of any serious safety concerns.

With these realistic examples of Faith in mind, does it seem convenient to apply similar reasoning to our thinking about God? Think of that for a minute. Here are some words from the Bible found in Hebrews 11:3. Here, take a look! It reads: "By faith, we understand that the universe was formed by God's command so that what is seen was not made out of what is visible." Can you imagine, that one opening verse of the Bible (Gen. 1:1) gives us a sweeping summary of the creation of our mysterious and magnificent universe. A creation produced, not by a Big Bang, but by the spoken word of an Omnipotent God? May I share with you a bite-size appetizer from the menu of mysteries that make up this marvelous God-created universe?

Did you know that what the learned scientists, now call the observed universe, is an admission that we human beings, even with the assistance of ingenious space probing devices like the Hubble Telescope deployed millions of miles into intergalactic space, can only glimpse at the farthest reaches of the observable universe? Despite this very limited view, it would be intellectually dishonest not to acknowledge the vast progress of science and technology enabling us to take a small peek through a narrow window into this amazing and ever expanding universe.

As you look up and scan the twinkling stars did you ever wonder how many worlds are floating out there in the endless distance of what seems to be an infinite dome? How far away these planets must be. Indeed, they are light-years (1 light year = approximately 6 trillion miles) away from our planet earth. Did you ever wonder – how are these mysteries of the heavens maintained with such precision? Day in, day out the international language of the heavens can be heard by every creature on earth. There is no place on earth or language of man where the wonder of this amazing universe does not baffle and overwhelm with awe the brightest minds. We need to pause to allow ourselves to think of the creative genius of this invisible God we discovered in our early Bible reference (Gen. 1:1). What do you think? Isn't that an amazing exercise of the mind – just thinking about cosmic drama? Since you seem so fascinated, let me share with you some basic information about the observed universe.

In the lingo of the astronomers or astrophysicists – galaxies are clusters of stars. Planets revolve around these stars that are kept in their respective orbits by powerful magnetic forces. The most recent count shows more than 200 billion galaxies. Within each galaxy, there are estimated over 100 billion plus stars. Our own Milky Way galaxy includes over 100 billion stars. For example, among these billions of stars in the Milky Way, is our SUN. Its satellite planets are: Mercury, Venus, Earth, Mars, Jupiter, Saturn, Uranus, Neptune and Pluto.

Oh yes! Planet Earth! – What a wonderful place! As we travel along together and run into these amazing eye-openers, we need to slow down and ponder some things about God that we let slip by because we have not spent enough time thinking about the genius of God in creation. For starters, have you thought that despite the trillions of miles that separate the galaxies and planets. Planet Earth in the Milky Way galaxy is the only known place, among all these billions and trillions of celestial bodies, where human life is sustainable? Science and technology will never give up trying to refute this mysterious reality. When you think of our position in the planetary system, think this: we are located about 93 million miles away from our sun. This is our source of heat and light. If we were a bit closer, we would fry to a crisp. If we were a bit further away we would freeze to solid ice. In God's intricate design, He has provided an infrastructure of heat, light and water in abundance to sustain our human existence and to cool the fiery core of the earth.

Have you thought of the hydrologic cycle that keeps all living creatures alive for a limited span of time? The water we consume daily comes from the cyclic motion of warm gases rising from the earth's surface to form clouds that later release these condensed gases in the form of rain that, as you know, is the prime source of life-saving hydration. Here is another of so many, many, evidences of the existence of God: Did you know that in the Bible (Genesis 2:7) we have a clear statement regarding the creation of man – from the dust of the ground? This fact was rarely disputed but was difficult to understand. As man became more "sophisticated" he kept probing the heavens above and the earth beneath. What has he found under his feet? He found that chemical and mineral components of the dust of the earth are all included and meticulously accounted for in the human body. The dust of the ground includes trace quantities of mercury, iron copper, zinc, calcium, magnesium, manganese, etc. When we end this excursion through **Thinking Wonderland** you may want to get a hold of Chemistry Periodic Table and be amused or amazed!

CHAPTER 4

THE OMNIPOTENT FACTOR

Can anyone do absolutely anything even beyond the unthinkable?

So what are you thinking? Isn't this Omnipotent God amazing? Hear the words of the Hebrew Prophet Isaiah speaking of God – "I have made the earth and created man upon it; I, even my hands have, stretched out the heavens, and all their host have I commanded" (Isaiah 45:12). If you are a believer listening in on our conversation, as we travel along, you have to be saying: Wow! God is full of wonder – He is indeed wonderful. He is indeed marvelous – He marvels all of us! He is awesome. He awes not just some of us but all of us! Just thinking about this Wonderful, Marvelous, Awesome God sends us into spiritual ecstasy. If you, my friend are not yet a believer, just let's keep thinking. As Robert Frost wrote, "We have promises to keep and miles to go before I sleep." As you can imagine, I have not even skimmed the surface of the cosmic wonder of God's mysterious universe. That is because of its immensity and complexity and also because, I must add, of my limited knowledge.

But are you ready for this? Now, let's briefly switch our focus from the mysterious heavens above to our unique planet earth (Terra-Firma). This uniquely marvelous piece of real estate is so incredibly located and strategically situated that it supports all forms of life that are not possible anywhere else among the billions of planets in the UNIVERSE. Has it ever occurred to you that this Omnipotent God we are thinking about, despite his unlimited power to do anything, anytime, anywhere, anyhow – whatever he makes and maintains – he does it in meticulous order and precision? For example, there exists a similar pattern between every conceivable thing that God has created in the heavens and upon the earth. These patterns are concealed, invisible, complex and, to say the least mysterious. Keep in mind as you think about these eye-popping, breath-taking, wonders of the world about us – nothing was originally created by man. **God, we believe, created them all!** Not a single grain of sand is unaccounted for, or a single leaf falling to the ground in the gentle autumn breeze. No grain of sand, no leaf of a tree escapes the effects of invisible gravity. Speaking of gravity – remember we mentioned that Bible verse (Job 32:8) stating that God inserts a spirit or "instinct" in man that enables him to see the invisible and understand the complexities of his creation.

Have you ever heard of Isaac Newton? (1642-1727) Newton was a premature, English baby boy born on Christmas Day. He was so tiny he could fit easily into a quart pot. So sickly, he was not expected to live past infancy. But live he did, and what he discovered changed our lives and brought about a revolution in the thinking of things that affect all our lives today. By unanimous agreement Isaac Newton was the greatest scientist of his time and – no apologies – of all times. **Isaac Newton,** the great genius of science was also by the way among other things – you ready for this – **A Born Again Christian!** With Newton's discovery of the universal laws of gravity, his famous three laws of motion, and the mathematics that explained these laws, he showed that every movement large or small on the ground, in water, in the air as well as the farthest reaches of space behave according to the same universal laws of gravity.

In his book – "Principa Mathematica" – the greatest science book ever written, he blew away the cloud of chaotic mystery that hung over the question of how the universe works. He showed in "Principa" that everything, everywhere behaves in an orderly and understandable way. These exceptional and ingenious insights were clearly the evidence of the Omnipotent God. Divine inspiration (referred to earlier) allowed the Thinking machine in Newton's brain and spirit to conceive and understand these complex relationships deeply encoded in these patterns of nature – out in space and on the ground. Newton believed that God allowed him to gain insight into areas of knowledge about His complex works and gave him the mental equipment to think, analyze and present them to a world that awaited his genius in order to progress its civilization. Before Newton there was no notion that the falling of an apple from a tree or the movement of fish in the sea, the fluttery of leaves in the wind had anything in common with the movement of the heavenly bodies we call stars, planets, etc.

NEWTON WAS THE FIRST TO SEE SIMILARITIES IN PHYSICAL LAWS GOVERNING THE HEAVENLY BODIES AND THE LAWS OF NATURE THAT CONTROL AND SUSTAIN OUR LIVES ON THIS EARTH.

Newton's ingenious discovery of the LAWS OF GRAVITY and his famous three laws of motion were earthshaking breakthroughs of all time. His insight into the universal laws and their mathematical models leaves those of us who are trained in the various disciplines of physical sciences, in perpetual awe as we think of his towering genius. Did you know with all the deserved adulation that was heaped upon Newton, he was the first to admit that he was only privileged to get a peek into the wonderland of God's creative genius! (Remember that Bible Verse: Gen. 1:1). Please keep in mind and never ever forget that Isaac Newton, that great Master Scientist did not or could not make or design a single law of nature. His genius remains engraved in history because a sovereign God rescued him from an infant demise and set him up to receive these mind boggling insights. Today over three centuries later our lives, our civilizations, depend almost entirely on the fundamentals of his original work.

Let's take a rest break; we have been covering a lot of ground using our thinking machine. While we are on rest break (because time is so valuable) let me share with you some ingenious things that Newton noticed. He insisted that every single movement in the universe can be analyzed mathematically, and he invented the tools to do just that. i.e., the two branches of mathematics – differential and integral calculus. With these tools it became possible not just to work out what was going on in all the motions of the universe, above or below, but to predict their orbits, their vectors – their magnitude and direction. I sense that our rest break is getting a little more Newtonian than I intended. Here are some other little secrets that Newton credited God for revealing to him i.e., showed him that gravity is at work in the lifting of a cup of tea/coffee, in the orbit of planet earth around its star (the sun), in the movement of a city bus on a city street, in the launching of a rocket, in the flying of an aircraft, in the sailing of a ship, even in walking down the street in the heat of the summer or in the chilly winter weather. In other words from the smallest molecule to the greatest planets – Newton's Laws (God's Law that he discovered) made it possible to predict the motion of everything in our dynamic universe.

Besides his discovery of the laws of gravity and his famous three laws of motion (Inertia, acceleration, reaction) and forces. Newton discovered some never before understood properties of light. He observed that light emanating from the rays of the sun had a lot to teach us. Remember earlier on we talked about **information IS WHERE YOU FIND IT?** I was not surprised and neither should you that Isaac Newton, our legendary genius took his cue for thinking about the mysterious nature of light from – The Holy Bible. Wow again! Looks like the Bible has everything in it. Taste and see or look and find! It was Alexander Pope who wrote the epitaph of Newton – "The world was in darkness and God said let there be light and there was Newton." The fact is that in Gen. 1:1 God said let there be light and there was this phenomenon we call light, without which there could be no existence of life on this earth. Newton's thinking led him to aim a light beam from the sun's ray, through a prism which refracted and revealed a spectrum of colors i.e., **R**ed, **O**range, **Y**ellow, **G**reen, **B**lue, **I**ndigo, **V**iolet (ROYGBIV). This discovery launched a spate of inquiry into the nature of light. The scientists of our time who delve into the complex area of Quantum Physics and the mathematics of quantity owe much of their basic knowledge to Sir. Isaac Newton whose life started as a frail infant, not expected to survive his childhood. Later in his youth, he was racked with two major breakdowns yet survived to leave us all a priceless legacy of scientific thinking and the related foundation mathematics.

Newton's work in mathematics and science has been the Holy Grail of Scientific Thinkers for over four centuries and will remain so for many generations to come. Even a late legendary physicist of the 20th century – Albert Einstein, has repeatedly said that if he were able to see a bit further into the mysteries of nature it was because he climbed upon the shoulders of the revered Isaac Newton.

We have been thinking, if we haven't lost our train of thought by dabbling a bit into the halls of science, about God's Omnipotence in creation – in the heavens and on planet earth. We have not even scratched the surface of the wonders of God's awesome creation – in the heavens and on planet earth. Regrettably, we must move on because we have a long journey ahead of us – but time passes so quickly. Let's think a bit about the next of the three attributes we touched on earlier, remember? They were God's Omnipotence, His Omniscience and His Omnipresence.

CHAPTER 5

THE OMNISCIENT FACTOR

Can Anyone Know Absolutely Everything?

So God's Omniscience! What does that mean, well, without the aid of a dictionary; we can extract or derive its meaning. Omni (refers only to God) and science refers to knowing and all knowledge. What is your thinking about the possibility or reality that God knows everyone, everything and every time – past, present and future – Wow! There we go again (from now on when we WOW let's think of WOW meaning – WONDER OF WONDERS). So what is your thinking about God's Omniscience? While you are sorting out your response let me ask you a friendly question. Do you really think that in the all-inclusive knowledge of God that he knows this very moment what we are thinking before we even talk about it? One more question to ponder as you sort out your answer to my questions about the Omniscience of God. Would it surprise you to know that we can get that answer from the information source (The Holy Bible) that inspired Sir Isaac Newton and many other intellectual giants that we will be talking about later on?

Before we talk further about this amazing topic of God's Omniscience, I should mention my self-imposed rule on assumptions. It says: The eleventh commandment is – THOU SHALL NOT ASSUME ANYTHING! I will not assume that you have read or are familiar with the Old Testament in the Bible (That's why I brought along a copy on our journey for our ready reference).

In the Old Testament God spoke to the ancient people of Israel through various events and phenomena, but frequently through prophets. These men were inspired (Holy men), and directed by God to convey specific messages of information and sometimes instructions to His people. One of these holy men was a prophet named Ezekiel. Here, let me show you a verse from one of Ezekiel's early prophesies (Ez. 11:5). It reads: "And the Spirit of the Lord fell upon me and said unto me, "This is what the Lord says: that is what you are saying, O house of Israel, **but I know every single thought that you are thinking."**

Can you ever imagine that? That is a statement of utmost clarity about the Omniscience of God. He knows everything about everyone not only people walking around like we are and talking about thinking but He knows about people before they were born – you mean pre-natal? Yes pre-natal. Is that in the Bible? Yes my friend – there are many examples stated in the Holy Bible. Let's flip over some pages from the Old Testament: look at this one (Jer. 1:5) from the Hebrew Prophet Jeremiah, it reads; "Before I formed you in the womb I knew you, before you were born, I set you apart, I appointed you as a prophet to the nations." While you were thinking about that amazing statement about God's Omniscience, let me show you another similar statement in the New Testament by a man named Paul. Ever heard of him? Well, this is a very strange and intriguing story. Before we read together from the Bible what he said about God's Omniscience let me brief you on this man referred to in the New Testament as the Apostle Paul. We are introduced to this man whose given name was Saul of Tarsus.

Saul grew up in Tarsus, a Roman colony off the Mediterranean Coast. He was a very religious Jew who later became a zealous rabbi. Josephus, a noted Roman Historian, writes that he lived around Jerusalem at the time of Jesus (if you recall we spoke about this God-man called Jesus of Nazareth earlier). Saul hated people, who in his eyes, were religious fanatics. These people were nicknamed "the way", because of their Faith in Jesus Christ who said He is the Way. Saul, we are told, was on his way from Jerusalem to Damascus (Syria) with religious authority to capture and extradite these religious fanatics to Jerusalem for trial. These people when arrested would be tried and penalized for what? For believing that Jesus is the Messiah, promised by God in the Old Testament Scriptures, to come in human form and provide salvation for all people. But did you hear what happened to Saul? Let me brief you from the text of Scripture in Acts Chapter 9. In summary, as he and his entourage were galloping from Jerusalem toward Damascus, suddenly, a light from heaven brighter than noon sun blinded him, and losing his balance he fell to the ground where he heard a voice calling his name twice: Saul, Saul, why are you persecuting me? Can you imagine his state of shock? he was petrified with fright and blurted out the questions: "Who are you Lord?" "What will you have me to do?" This is one of the most intriguing stories of New Testament Scripture. You can read it from the Bible I have been sharing with you at the start of our journey.

I must make a few points about the Apostle Paul before getting to the point of his statement regarding the Omniscience of God. (Gal. 1:15-16). In the story (Acts 9) this man called Saul later referred to as Paul, had an amazing life changing experience of spiritual conversion when he was temporarily deprived of this sight and was later energized, empowered and enabled by the Holy Spirit. Woops. Remind me to explain THE HOLY SPIRIT later. Paul went out to become one of the greatest preachers of the Gospel – the good news of salvation. He became, beyond any doubt, the greatest teacher of New Testament Doctrines or teachings. I know you would like to hear more about Paul (we can do that later if you are interested) but now I'd like to show you a couple of verses from Paul's writings that exemplify the fact of God's ALL INCLUSIVE knowledge (Omniscience) of us even before we were born: Here Paul states in the verses of Gal. 1:15-16, "But when God, who set me apart from birth, and called me by His grace He was pleased to reveal His Son in me, that I might preach Him among the gentiles — -." As we think about God's Omniscience, here is one that will really fascinate you. I learned from my reading of Scripture that God not only knows everything, everywhere but that he is looking all the time. This Bible verse (Prov. 15:3) here it says: "The eyes of the Lord are in every place beholding the evil and the good." Wow! Did you think all that information was in the Bible? Do you have an interest in numbers and their precision?

Well here is one I'll leave you with before we move to our next conversation about the third attribute of God I mentioned earlier – His Omnipresence.

Have you ever heard of Peter, one of the disciples of Jesus, who was a fisherman when Jesus recruited him to be one of the twelve selected to become Key Movers and Shakers? It was a new era of thinking and believing (Faith) what God was doing in the lives of people who accepted the Lord Jesus as Savior. Let's hold that for later.

This Galilean fisherman, Peter, had a good heart, a quick wit and a very active mouth. He even volunteered to go to jail and if necessary die for his Master. But, Peter was one who we may call a blurter – quick to talk ahead of his thinking – quick to do things before he thought of what to do. From the story to which I will refer briefly you will notice that Jesus knew much more about Peter than he knew about himself. That's not all! Jesus had precise knowledge about what Peter would say and how many times he would say what he did not know he would say! Wow! Where is that information? Well where do you guess? The Bible of course. Here is the situation: Jesus is nearing the end of His ministry on earth. He is about to be captured and later crucified on a Roman cross. Subsequently (three days later) the Omnipotence of God was displayed in the miraculous, mysterious resurrection of an Immortal Savior of mankind. Let's get back to Peter. Before the tragic episode of Jesus' death, Jesus clearly stated that Peter would deny any association with Him. Peter vociferously insisted – No way would he deny his beloved Master! Here are the words of Jesus to Peter: (Luke 22:34). "I am telling you, Peter, the rooster shall not crow once this day before you will deny me three times this day." If we read Luke 22: 54-62, you will notice verse 57 says that "and he (Peter) denied Him, saying, woman, I know Him not. Verse 60, look at this sequence after three denials – "and Peter said, man, I know not what thou sayest, and immediately, while he yet spoke the rooster crew. Verse 61 really rivets the point. It says right here: "and the Lord turned and looked upon Peter. And Peter remembered the word of the Lord, how he had said unto him, before the rooster crows, you will deny me <u>three times.</u>" How is that for numerical precision?

What a story! It seems that Peter remembered what <u>we should also remember!</u> What's that? That there is one above us and beyond us, one who knows precisely all of our thoughts and our actions ahead of our time. This divine person we have been thinking about captures our thinking because His attributes escape our intellect. It seems, as we said before, we need faith (will talk about that later) to connect our Thinking about this mysterious God.

Now let's take another rest break – we have been covering a lot of territory as we stroll along in **Thinking Wonderland.** I can see from your expression that you are very engaged in our conversation. I can see that you have been thinking quite differently than when we started strolling together. My guess is that you have been filtering some thoughts as I shared them with you. You may be filtering these thoughts philosophically, intellectually, culturally, psychologically, historically metaphysically or even spiritually. I must tell you, I appreciate your attention and willingness to continue this very fascinating dialogue on Thinking about God – most importantly at this point or sometime later you should be asking yourself what am I really thinking about God?

CHAPTER 6

THE OMNIPRESENT FACTOR

*Is it possible to be ever present
everywhere at the same time?*

Now after a well deserved break, let's think together about the third attribute of God I mentioned earlier – His Omnipresence. Perhaps, a good start would be to define it; describe it; and then discuss and think about it together. This one is not so easy, but we will give it a whirl. His Omnipresence means being present everywhere at the same time. For example, we are strolling through this peaceful, tranquil "imaginary" wonderland of thinking (imaginary for our purpose) but we physically cannot be anywhere else at this moment. We are bound by these two coordinates of time and place.

If you recall we started our conversation, both of us enthralled and amazed at the creative genius of God. We acknowledged that He is the creator of everything – the heavenly bodies, and all earthly substance as well as the laws of nature that control them. Did you know that most of these natural laws are invisible to our eyes and also to all kinds of ingenious optical devices? Think of the most universal of all laws that control our lives – **Gravity**. This is a good example for our discussion of **Omnipresence** because **Gravity is everywhere at the same time and no one can ever see it.** By the way, let me share with you the scientific **definition of Gravity.** It is the invisible <u>force</u> that pulls all unsupported bodies towards the earth's center with an ever increasing velocity. What has the definition of gravity got to do with the Omnipresence of God? I told you this one is not going to be easy to sort out, but hang on!

In the first analysis the God of the Bible tells us quite a bit about Himself by the "things" he created. Keep in mind also that the laws he created are subject to his control but He the creator is not subject to their influence or control. Now we have built a clear and stepwise logical case for under-standing what scripture informs us about the Omnipresence of God. The examples I will share with you will show that, unlike gravity, which operates invisibly everywhere on the planet, it only does one thing and one thing only. It just keeps pulling and pulling down anything unsupported toward the earth's center. Even as we speak gravity is keeping us from flying off into space by invisibly and silently pulling us toward the "ground" so we can keep walking. So, gravity is omnipresent, but it can only do one-thing all the time "everywhere" i.e. pull down anything unsupported, (hang on to your cap or else) listen to this – once we leave the earth's magnetic field of gravity – gravity is out of business. This brings us back to our prior statement that **only God is omnipresent!** Now let me **share** with you a Bible story or two that will really show you the reality and power of God's Omnipresence, and then we will both kick around some thinking about it.

Ever heard of the Biblical story of **Jonah and the whale?** By the way, please know that this is not just the tale of a whale or the whale of a tale. This is real time information about Jonah, (a prophet of God) who received specific instructions from God regarding a specific mission but decided to do **his thing his way** – the Frank Sinatra principle you might say. Here is a sketch of the Bible narrative that, you will agree, clearly illustrates **the Omnipresence of God** that we are thinking about.

The book of Jonah has four short chapters. All of them keep telling us that we cannot get away from the presence of an Omnipresent God, whether we run, fly or swim, God is everywhere. In the story, Jonah was instructed to leave his home base and head for Nineveh, the ancient capital of the Assyrian Empire. Jonah did not care for the Ninevites because of their reputation for evil practices. God told Jonah to take a message of warning to that great but wicked city. But look at this verse 3 in the first chapter of Jonah. It says, **"But Jonah ran away from the presence of the Lord** (so he thought) and headed for Tarshish (a Western Mediterranean city off the coast of Spain.) Look at this, Jonah's overland trip to Tarshish was almost 500 miles northeast of his point of departure. Instead of going east, he proceeded in a direction about 2000 miles to the west to get away from God and the Ninevites. He boarded a ship bound for Tarshish. He planned this 2000 mile trip to **get away from the presence of the Lord.** The story goes on, and in the verses that follow, we are told that God, who controls all that he created including, wind, sea and sea creatures etc., stirred up the wind causing a great tempest to shake up the ship to near destruction with Jonah aboard.

The frightened angry mariners tried to find some relief from the merciless tempest pounding their ship. Where was Jonah? Can you believe this? Jonah was asleep in some remote place on the ship. The next thing we hear is that these superstitious sailors cast lots and Jonah was the one who was selected to be thrown overboard into the raging sea. The story says that God prepared a great fish (whale) to swallow Jonah. There, in the belly of this great fish for three days and three nights, Jonah miraculously survived the lethal effects of the digestive acids in the whale's belly. These acid fluxes could perforate iron or steel. After Jonah's recognition that being in the belly of the great fish did not remove him from the presence and power of God, you can imagine how sincerely he prayed. God heard his prayer (chapter 2:10) and caused the fish to eject Jonah to shore-side. You could say that God arranged a submarine ride to get him to Nineveh and a rocket launch to get him on the beach. Finally, in the third chapter of the story we find Jonah following his original instructions to take the message of warning to Nineveh. The people repented and God's judgment was averted. Jonah learned from this experience that the Omnipresent God is in the heaven, on land, on sea, everywhere doing different things all at once. He also learned that God can reach us anywhere as he wishes. THERE IS NO HIDING PLACE BEYOND HIS REACH! In Jonah's case – He, God was not beyond the reach of Jonah's prayer despite his submersion in the horrible and lethal chemistry of a whale's belly. So what do you think of Jonah and his escape plan? We sure learned that the Omnipresent God is never absent anywhere and cannot be escaped anytime!

Remember earlier on we talked about that legendary King David who was observing the starry heavens and expressing his amazement at the Omnipotence of God expressed in the mystery of the heavens? King David, besides being a famous king and keen observer, was also a careful and curious thinker. Let me flip over in our handy reference Bible and let's look together at what King David thought about the Omnipresence of God. Here in Ps. 139: 7-12: reads "Where can I go from your Spirit? Where can I flee from your presence? If I go up to the heavens, you are there. If I make my bed in the depths, you are there. If I rise on the wings of the dawn, you are there. If I settle on the far side of the sea, even there your hand will guide me; your right hand will hold me fast. If I say, "surely the darkness will hide me and the light become night around me, even the darkness will not be dark to you. The night will shine as the day for darkness is as light to you."

If we summarize David's thinking – you might conclude that his bottom line was that there is just no conceivable place in the heavens above or upon the earth below where God is not present! There is one more example of the Omnipresence of God that I cannot resist sharing with you as an illustration. Do you recall when we started our stroll through **Thinking Wonderland;** I mentioned Jesus of Nazareth and His words and miraculous works? We will be sharing much more exciting things about Him later. For now, let me set the stage for this famous statement that he made about His Omnipresence.

The New Testament includes four Gospels; Matthew, Mark, Luke and John. All four gospels capture events featuring Jesus' Ministry over a period of about three years. At the end of this time, true to prophetic fulfillment, Jesus was crucified by the Roman authorities in collusion with Jewish religious leaders. The strangest thing happened, have you heard this? Three days after He was buried in a sealed tomb – He arose immortal! Following this unprecedented resurrection – He spent forty days moving around the Jerusalem area interacting with his disciples. Listen to this: on the fortieth day he gathered these faithful followers and said these words. Let's flip over in the New Testament and find His words in the 28th chapter of Matthew, verses 18-20. Let's read out loud: "And Jesus came and spake unto them, saying, All power is given unto me in heaven and in earth. Go ye therefore, and teach all nations, baptizing them in the name of the Father, and of the Son, and of the Holy Ghost: Teaching them to observe all things whatsoever I have commanded you: and, lo, <u>I am with you always,</u> even unto the end of the age."

By the way, the words we have just read together have been labeled The Great Commission. This statement made by the Lord Jesus has been resource and recourse for courage and confidence in THE PURSUITS of countless missionaries. They have, since these words were spoken, taken the message of the Gospel of Christ literally to the ends of the earth. This Gospel message has been the battle cry of missionaries from all imaginable nations and people groups for over two thousand years. As we will discuss later, this Gospel message of God's grace, hope, peace and love has impacted the world view shared by most of our civilization up to and through our post-modern period. These courageous people of faith could, by their own admission, never have achieved the near impossible missionary work, including martyrdom, if they did not deeply believe in the Omnipresence of God – they did not think that there was a solitary moment when a divine presence did not surround them!

I'd like to make an honest admission to you on the subject of God's Omnipresence. Strange as it may seem – Omnipresence being everywhere at the same time is tough enough to digest, but to me the most baffling is the concept of God's <u>invisible</u> presence. What helps me in better conceptualizing this spiritual phenomenon is a statement by the Lord Jesus in John's Gospel Chapter 4:24. This verse says: "God is a Spirit and they who worship Him must worship Him in spirit and in truth." This means, as Spirit, God is not limited to or bound by time and space. Does that help you understand the Omnipresence of God! It sure was helpful to me. With this rest break coming up in a few minutes, I must say how pleased I am that you have kept your promise when I invited you to join me on this extended stroll through **Thinking Wonderland.** You are hanging in! It even looks like you are getting very comfortable with thinking about God, about matters of faith, (in your lingo, you may call them metaphysics) and more specifically we spent some time thinking about what I referred to as the big **three Os:** God's Omnipotence, God's Omniscience and God's Omnipresence.

We sure covered a lot of areas of thought exchange. As we come up to another break we can relax and reflect on some of the topics of thought we shared together. Have you thought of the wonderful opportunity that we embraced by breaking away from the technology clatter and clutter of the ubiquitous digital computer, Television, DVDs, Radio, MP3s, IPOD, smart phones, etc. in order to treat ourselves to some real quality thinking? As we will see later after the break when we resume our stroll through **Thinking Wonderland,** what we are thinking about are items of thought that transcend all other material and temporary topics. These are **matters of faith that reach up** to God and these are **matters of the attributes of God that reach down to us.**

Are you surprised that we can talk about God and how we think about Him in such a non-threatening and amicable way? Briefly, think of God who is Omnipotent; (created and controls all things, places and people) Omniscient (knows all things about all places, things and people) and Omnipresent – although invisible appears everywhere doing different things at the same time. WOW! Can't wait, after digesting all this was going to say theological stuff – logical thought we will be ready, eager and even animated with desire to wade further out into the streams of more refreshing thoughts. We will break now. You tell me when you have mulled over and sorted out some of our discussions. Here, you can use my Bible during the break. While you are relaxing, remember I mentioned that in the Gospel Jesus instructed His disciples to go and preach worldwide. Think of this good news message as God communicating with us about our need for a Savior. He has provided that Savior in the person of His Son the Lord Jesus Christ. The message includes specific instructions regarding what to do to receive God's eternal salvation. It really sounds too simple to be true – but it is very true. Just flip over in the New Testament in Romans 10:9 it reads: That if thou shalt confess with thy mouth the Lord Jesus, and shalt believe in thine heart that God hath raised him from the dead, thou shalt be saved and verse 13 reads For whosoever shall call upon the name of the Lord shall be saved. I am going to relax a bit and you do the same – but in your quiet moments – keep THINKING, THINKING.

As you wind down, during the rest break, here is what I think you may be thinking: "This stimulating, provocative conversation is like a **can of peanuts** that I sometimes use to test my will power. I say – "I will only munch a few of these nuts and that's it!" In a few minutes I begin to wonder where the peanuts went. When we resume our conversation as we continue our stroll through **Thinking Wonderland,** you will **wonder where the time went.** So, let's get going because we have promises to keep and miles to go before we sleep.

PART 2

WHAT ARE YOU THINKING ABOUT MAN?

THE MANY SIDES OF THE SAME COIN

CHAPTER 7

WHO IS THIS MAN?

What a piece of work is man

William Shakespeare the world famous English playwright and poet in one of his classic tragedies (Hamlet) coined this expression reflecting the mystery of man – "what a piece of work is man." Another legend of an earlier time – a Hebrew King who was also a poet and author of many Biblical Psalms repeatedly exclaimed – "What is man that God is mindful of him?" Then there was this other conundrum of a statement – the child is the father of the man. Man is a mystery!

As we continue our stroll through **Thinking Wonderland** we may surprise ourselves at the complexity of our personal origin, the adventure of our history and the contradictions of our humanity – our own nature! Let me start by sharing with you some brief but fascinating thoughts about man – generic man – homo-sapiens species.

Everyone (ourselves included) sees each other through the windows of our souls – our natural eyes. Here is a curious thought – everyone of us has a philosopher within. Oh – seems we are getting into some heavy stuff! No not at all – when we break it down it will become surprisingly logical, factual, reasonable, enjoyable and even believable. For starters – let's clear up the philosophy part and maybe we will come back to it later if you are curious. For our conversation, we will think of philosophy as: <u>everyone's instinctive thinking about the puzzling issues of life, and seeking satisfying answers.</u> We do this all the time – it helps us in coping with the curve balls that life throws at us. For example: If I think positively or negatively about events in life – I am perceived as a person who sees the water glass half full or half empty. That is a powerful philosophy to guide our thinking and consequently our actions

If you are a half-full thinker – you will think positively and act courageously. If you are a half-empty thinker you will think negatively and act timidly or tentatively. In other words your negative thoughts will embrace negative outcomes. The late Dr. Norman Vincent Peale left us a legacy of popular expression: The power of positive thinking! In his book he encouraged his readers to think positively. Are you getting my drift that we are all, at the core of being, Thinkers? We do unconsciously what our current excursion through **Thinking Wonderland** is all about. We keep thinking in the direction of the bent of our minds and the temperament of our emotions.

A few thoughts from the archives of poetry may add a soothing flavor to our thinking about Man vs. Man. Edwin Markham, after seeing Millet's world famous painting of a brutalized toiler – wrote his world famous poem – "THE MAN WITH THE HOE." Here are a few excerpts from his poem:

> *Bowed by the weight of centuries he leans Upon*
> *his hoe and gazes on the ground,*
> *The emptiness of ages in his face,*

And on his back, the burden of the world.
Who made him dead to rapture and despair,
A thing that grieves not and that never hopes,
Stolid and stunned, a brother to the ox?
Who loosened and let down this brutal jaw?
Whose was the hand that slanted back this brow?
Whose breath blew out the light within this
brain?
Is this the Thing the Lord God made and gave
To have dominion over sea and land;
To trace the stars and search the heavens for
power;
To feel the passion of Eternity?
Is this the dream He dreamed who shaped the
suns
And marked their ways upon the ancient deep?
Down all the caverns of Hell to their last gulf
There is no shape more terrible than this—
More tongued with cries against the world's blind
greed—
More filled with signs and portents for the soul—
More packed with danger to the universe.
O masters, lords and rulers in all lands,
How will the future reckon with this Man?
How answer his brute question in that hour
When whirlwinds of rebellion shake all shores?
How will it be with kingdoms and with kings—
With those who shaped him to the thing he is—

When this dumb Terror shall rise to judge the world,

After the silence of the centuries?

That was Edwin Markham's view, through his eyes, of man in a distressed and exploited condition. You might say Markham saw the glass half empty not half full. Now listen to Sam Walter Foss in his poem titled: "THE HOUSE BY THE SIDE OF THE ROAD".

Let me live in a house by the side of the road,

Where the race of men go by;

The men who are good and the men who are bad,

As good and as bad as I.

I would not sit in the scorner's seat,

Or hurl the cynic's ban;

Let me live in a house by the side of the road

And be a friend to man.

I see from my house by the side of the road,

By the side of the highway of life,

The men who press with the ardor of hope,

The men who are faint with the strife.

But I turn not away from their smiles nor their tears

Both parts of an infinite plan;

Let me live in my house by the side of the road

And be a friend to man.

Let me live in my house by the side of the road

Where the race of men go by;

They are good, they are bad, they are weak, They are strong,
Wise, foolish so am I.
Then why should I sit in the scorner's seat
Or hurl the cynic's ban? -
Let me live in my house by the side of the road
And be a friend to man.

Wow! Nothing like a fragrant whiff of poetry to stimulate our thinking. "Let me live in a house by the side of the road and be a friend to man." You might say Foss saw the glass half full not half empty.

Edwin Markham's view of the Man with the Hoe and Sam Foss's view of the Man from his perch in a House by the side of the Road – gracefully escort us into our thinking about the nature of man and what makes him tick. What makes him behave the way he does toward his fellow man – the good in him, the bad in him, the love in him, the hate in him, the genius in him, and the folly in him! No wonder the poet wrote from his musings about man – "What a piece of work is man!"

CHAPTER 8

THE ORIGIN OF MAN

Where do we find this information?

How's your recall? Remember earlier when we started this thinking conversation we shared a sound bite **Information IS WHERE YOU FIND IT.** We accepted the premise that the Bible provided reliable information about the origins of all things as well as the basis for tracing all things created to a Divine Creator. This divine creator we reasoned is alone worthy of the attributions of Omnipotence (can do all things); Omniscience (knows all things); and Omnipresence (is everywhere at all times). This is important to recall because where else can we find reliable and credible information about the origin of this complex and mysterious species we call – Man? By the way, the search for man's origin is an age-old quagmire that could ruin our thinking adventure. I know you were waiting for me to bring up Charles Darwin the high priest of Evolution Of The Species, or more recently, Richard Dawkins' infamous book – The God Delusion. Since you prefer for me to skip over Darwin and Dawkins – I will.

If you don't mind we can find reliable information conveniently inscribed in this copy of the Bible that I brought along, in my backpack, for ready reference. So, let's take a look at what the Bible says about the creation of this Man. It says here in Genesis, Chapter 2 Verse 7 "And the Lord God formed man of the dust of the ground, and breathed in him the breath of life; and man became a living soul!!" It further says in verses 8 and 9 that God placed this man in a green environment and instructed him in farming and landscaping and the freedom to eat of every tree except one. The tree of the Knowledge of good and evil. (Verses 16 & 17) Take a look closely here: warning instructions were bold and clear. If he ate of that forbidden tree – labeled **good and evil** – he would surely die. Later in verses 21 & 22 of Genesis Chapter 2 we read that God formed a woman from the side of the man to be by his side as his companion. This, admittedly, is a simplified version of the creation of man, and in fact – how and where he originated.

If you agree, we can defer or avoid the contentious and spurious argument against the origin of our species by the creative acts of God we discussed earlier. If you further agree, we can continue a thoughtful and logical conversation about this mysterious creature we call MAN! Did you ever think that one way to prove a point, beyond even the logic of the most passionate argument, is by observing results predicted based on cause(s)? In other words, the proof of the pudding is really in the eating. Remember, oh yes, how could you forget? We just observed, by poetic revere, that in reality, Man's history presents him as sometimes – good – very good and other times – bad – very bad! We will discuss these realities as we keep moving along in **Thinking Wonderland.** The question is where did this duality in man's nature come from? What makes this same man so good at one time and so bad at other times? These were the thoughts of the man in the "House by the side of the Road" as he watched men go by, he noticed that some were good and some as bad as he was.

This mysterious duality in man derived from his disobedience of God's specific instructions to stay away from any contact with that singular tree of the knowledge of Good and Evil in the Garden of Eden. This as you recall was both literal and symbolic. That's what we read in the Good Book. I believe that, do you? OK! Now based on the logic I mentioned earlier regarding the proof of the pudding – or cause and effect and even if you doubted that God created mankind and that his disobedience switched man's pristine/innocent nature to a dual personality with the capacity for good and evil you should be curious. This point deserves repetition because while we may not completely grasp the mystery of his duality perhaps our insight from the Holy Bible may help lift the fog of controversy about man's nature that has prevailed since the dawn of time.

Let me share with you from a page of my personal habits, a graphic picture of man's duality that I found inexpressively vivid. I am an early riser (are you?). Regardless of where I am, at home, or abroad I am up early enough to out-race the sun. In other words, I am in the outdoors before the sun sheds its first gleam of light. In the shadows of the early morning, I enjoy just gazing up above for an awesome search of the starry heavens. I am just so thrilled when occasionally I catch a close glimpse of that life-size fluorescent disc – the moon. I watch this full moon really amazed that with my unaided eyes I can see this beautiful heavenly light – 240,000 miles away gleaming from the star-sprinkled skies. Another morning, I look up again, and what do I see? I see only one half of that same silvery moon shining down on me. I stand there in utter amazement as I see the other half of the moon in total darkness. I can't see the other half but I know it's there. The moon, at this time, is in the first quarter of its orbital rotation around the earth – and it is hiding its dark side and showing its bright or <u>light side</u>.

What a display of natural drama in the heavens! This, my friend, was truly mesmerizing and an unforgettable impression of <u>man's duality</u> One side bright light and at the same time, the other side dark as night. This personal graphic moon-gazing was a powerful illustration to me of the mysterious dual nature of man. His light side and his dark side. I can see from the curious look on your face that my early morning moon-gazing fascination has engaged you. So are we now ready to descend from the moonlit – starry heavens to planet earth where dwell our "fellowmen." This too is a fascinating and even more complex drama. Where would you like to start thinking about the duality of man as he relates to his fellowman? Somehow and for some reason Sam Walton Foss's poem – The House by the Side of the Road – we read earlier rings a clear bell to our thinking. Remember these lines:

> *Let me live in a house by the side of the road,*
> *Where the race of men go by;*
> *The men who are good and the men who are bad,*
> *As good and as bad as I.*
> *I would not sit in the scorner's seat,*
> *Or hurl the cynic's ban;*
> *Let me live in a house by the side of the road*
> *And be a friend to man.*

Again, I let you chose to kick off the thinking excursion. Do you want to apply the view of the glass half full – man's good side or the glass half empty – man's bad side? So you want me to go first! Ok, I'll oblige. I'll start looking at the half full – <u>man's good side.</u> As we think together about the spate of good things "man" has done and is doing for the benefit of others, it is a logical fact that there must be some thinking behind his actions. We are going to be trading questions back and forth about this mystery of man's duality! Are you excited? Good! Let's keep at it. Here is our first question, what is the trigger for his "good" side? Look at this: In the creation story we read here, take a look: In Genesis Chapter 1:27 it says God created man in His image and after His likeness.

CHAPTER 9

THE STRANGE DUALITY OF MAN

His good side and his bad side

Earlier we read that God formed man out of the earth and breathed in him the breath of life and man became alive (living soul). Let's slow down here this is a pivotal point in our conversation.

The Good Book is the primary source and the "grist" for the "mill" of our conversation. Remember that verse in Job 32:8 we cited earlier? "There is a Spirit in man and the inspiration of the Almighty gives him understanding?" That is the key, my friend – Now let us carefully turn this key together so we can get through the door of understanding a little bit about the <u>good side of man</u> – like the bright side of that first quarter mesmerizing moon at early dawn we both reveled in earlier. You see, God has ingeniously designed patterns in the universe of Nature. Patterns in the billions of planets and stars far, far away and patterns – amazing patterns embedded in things and people right here on planet earth. We, human beings, have been patterned by God, we are programmed to reflect God's likeness. Now the big question pops up (been popping up for ages) why are we good sometimes and bad other times? Remember that "key" we started turning together as we raised these insightful questions? Let's give it another turn as we ask the question again – why is man not good all the time – to himself and to others? Here is a possible answer – are you ready for this? Because God in His ingenious wisdom created man with the freedom to choose. This is a key thought! We will need it sooner and later!

Since we are going to be sharing some thoughts about Man vs. Man and his duality of good and evil we will keep our promise to define the term used in our conversation. So, let's define "good." For our purposes we will simply say: Good derives from thinking that urges a person(s) to care for others; to be concerned about others in some state of need; to show compassion for others and to find creative ways to help others at the expense of personal convenience and comfort. Is that a good definition of good? Good! I think so too. While we are at it, let's craft a definition of evil or bad. Bad (evil) derives from **thinking** that urges a person(s) to inflict or impact others causing distress, disarray discomfort and sometimes even death. Have you noticed, that for each definition, the single source from which the stream of duality of both good and evil flows is – our thinking? Ever heard the Chinese proverb that says: a picture is worth a thousand words? Well, let's make up our own proverb that says: "a few illustrations are worth a ten-thousand words." Want to talk first about some good people? Would you like to start by illustrating a few good people? You want me to go first? Ok I'll start. I started thinking of some really good people whose memories are buried in the archives of ancient history.

In my struggle to be fair in listing them in the category of good – I took a pass! My exception is the exception of ONE MAN WHO EPITOMIZED the ultimate **good in man.** Who might that be? Is that your question? Remember when we started this stroll through **Thinking Wonderland** I introduced a man called Jesus of Nazareth who walked the streets of Galilee and its environs followed by His disciples and sometimes large crowds. In one of His conversations, He stated that there is none <u>good</u> but <u>ONE</u>. In His inimitable way He was referring to Himself. The best I can do is to think of a few more contemporary individuals who unlike, Jesus of Nazareth, are mere mortals and are at best doing what good they can. They are like the shining lights on a hill.

In thinking about good people, or people driven to do good, we will think only of people who fit the definition we scripted. People who care less for themselves and more about others. These people focus on those who are less fortunate and who need care and personal attention and compassionate assistance. In other words, people who are always ready to lend a helping hand – even when their own hands are hurting or shackled by personal challenge. Ever heard of people called missionaries? These are committed and dedicated people who are usually driven by a deep conviction that exist to reach out to others in need of all kinds of help. You might say they hear a call (heard only by their ears) from places where they know that by going there a difficult and rigorous and even dangerous life awaits them. These good people all say without exception – I must answer the call.

These missionary types have a common credo. They say their credo comes from the Good Book –The Holy Bible. Another hallmark of these messengers of mercy is that they have no motivation to receive any personal rewards. Have you heard of the many physicians, teachers, nurses, craftsmen/women, etc who have been irresistibly urged to leave comfortable living behind and reach out to the needy and destitute. They venture into the most remote and inconvenient places in order to do some good for people they don't know – sometimes they don't even have a clue what these people look like.

When you raise the puzzling question – "what motivates these actions of love, mercy and compassion?" These missionaries usually quote the words of Jesus who said: "Go you therefore and teach all nations, baptizing them in the name of the Father, and of the Son and of the Holy Spirit. Teaching them to observe all things whatsoever I have commanded you and, lo, I am with you always, even unto the end of the world" (Matt. 28: 19-20) In addition to these Bible verses, known as the Great Commission, they sometimes refer to another verse in the New Testament: "As you have opportunity, do good to all men, especially those of the household of faith" (Gal. 6:10).

CHAPTER 10

THE SHINING LIGHTS OF MAN

The light of their thoughts and deeds
shines on and on

n August 26th 2010, the world paid post-humus tribute to Agnes Gonxha Bojaxhiu, a Roman Catholic nun from Albania, who belonged to a group she later founded called "Missionaries of Charity." Mother Teresa, as she was respectfully and affectionately known worldwide, repeatedly said that she was a "little pencil" in the hand of God who, through her, was sending love letters to the world. Well she was some "pencil" and she wrote enduring and endearing love letters to the world by the good she selflessly did in helping the helpless victims of poverty and human deprivation.

No wonder she won the Noble Prize in 1979 for her incredible sacrificial deeds of love and mercy towards the diseased, distressed, and the severely downtrodden peoples of India – especially her missions of mercy in Calcutta. The humanitarian work of Mother Teresa, this tiny and frail looking lady with a great heart of love for her fellow-pilgrims gave herself non-stop in a ministry she started 1959 in India. She was also a torch bearer in a worldwide propagation of the model of self-sacrifice which was at the core of her missionary credo.

Enough cannot be said about, Mother Teresa, this human machine of good deeds, love, kindness and caring for the poor. The movement she started has spread to many parts of the world, including the former Soviet Union (Russia), Eastern Europe, Asia, Africa and Latin America. These agents of mercy extend their helping hands to victims of natural disasters e.g., floods, earthquakes, famine, and refugee assistance. They rely solely on charity for funding and receive no pay or rewards of any kind. Mother Teresa couldn't wait to receive the Nobel Prize money when she publicly stated "This money is to be spent for the poor, every penny of it."

By the 1990's there were over a million co-workers in forty (40) countries following the lead and example set by Mother Teresa. She repeatedly stated that her work was modeled after Jesus of Nazareth who, in his heart, cared for the poor and with His voice and with His hands healed their diseases. For a very long time in the future Mother Teresa's name and work will be remembered and mentioned in the same sentence with those before her who cared for the poor and needy.

Although Mother Teresa and Albert Schweitzer were vastly different in background and pedigree, they certainly belong in the same paragraph in the history of people whose thinking was about doing good for others with little or no thought of personal sacrifice.

Albert Schweitzer, the Alsatian (German) born medical doctor, musician and theologian was the beneficiary of favorable nurturing that contributed to his intellectual accomplishments. As many others before him, he persisted in the onward march of his missionary aspirations THINKING about people in need. He surrendered to the compelling urge to go and help the helpless and those who seem hopeless. In 1917 Dr. Schweitzer founded a hospital in Lambaréné (French Equatorial Africa) and spent the rest of his life serving the village people as physician and surgeon. He was also Pastor of village churches, Village Chief, Super for buildings, Writer and a host of other hats that he wore. He died in 1965 at the age of ninety (90), and was buried in Lambaréné. Albert Schweitzer's deeds of mercy, kindness, love and the generosity of his heart lives on, because this man at some strategic moment in his life took some time to THINK about others whose burdens of poverty, sickness and distress he could help to relieve.

There are so many others who like the good doctor have left us an indelible memory of what can result from treasured moments of Thinking about doing something good for others!

Some of those other missionaries you may have heard of are: David Livingstone; William Carey; Adoniram Judson; John Wesley, Hudson Taylor and others of the past centuries. More recently, some of those you may have also heard of are: Jim Elliott and Frank Nate Saint (Missionary Aviation); Robert Pierce (World Vision); George Verwer (Operation Mobilization) et al. Then there are numerous missionary groups such as: Doctors Without Borders; Missionary Aviation Fellowship; Samaritan Purse; Mercy Ships; Salvation Army and America's Keswick and the list goes on. The list of these exceptional people who have dedicated their lives to bring a gleam of light in the darkness of unspeakable suffering of soul and body is quite lengthy. Nearly all of my information on these people comes from my reading about their work. No amount of reading can give a worthy glimpse into the personalities of these thinkers. Their passion is to see lives changed through the amazing grace of a merciful God.

As we speak, two of these exceptional people come to mind like – George Verwer of Operation Mobilization and Bill Welte of

Americas Keswick. They have crossed my path and left a lasting impression on me. The story of George Verwer can be read in so many books (e.g., OUT OF THE COMFORT ZONE) reports, and web sketches written about him. Let me share a snippet of my meeting and fellowship with "George" as he is affectionately called by O.M.ers (short for devotees of Operation Mobilization). I first heard about O.M. from Hoise Birks, a passionate missions-minded member of our congregation at the Galilee Gospel Chapel in Queens, New York. I met George and his "disciple" at an unforgettable dinner meeting in our home. We remained amazed from our first greeting followed by an evening's worth of praise-the-Lord-conversations as we listened to what God was doing in the world of missions – via George and his team of dedicated co-workers.

After they drove away into the cold and windy winter's night, our hearts were warmed as we reflected on story after story that George told us about how he came to faith and how he was called and led to world missions. He told us of this praying Christian lady from his home-town community in Wyckoff, New Jersey who, while he was in High School, not only ambushed him by her prayers but gave him a copy of John's Gospel. Later he came to faith in Christ after hearing a Gospel message preached by Billy Graham at the Madison Square Garden in New York. From here on, with world missions on his mind and in his thinking, after graduation from college, he landed at Moody Bible Institute to prepare for what would become the consuming passion of his life – bringing the life-changing message of salvation to all nations! George later teamed up Dale Rhoton (his college friend) and others to kick off his vision in Mexico and then on to Spain, then on to India. Then, the biggest vision of all – more like mission impossible – George saw (vision) a Ship! – to take missions teams world-wide with the same message that changed his life. This dynamo of a man, and his team, is evidence that, one person thinking possibilities and thinking God, can cast a vision of impossibility that turns into possibilities, that turns into reality right before your eyes! It seems that God can do anything with people who hear, answer His call, and are ready to go where He sends them and do what He leads them to do.

In October, 2009 at George Verwer and Dale Rhoton's invitation, I flew to Barbados, W.I. where I boarded the Logos Hope (one of the ships in George's early vision – they were three (3) of them). As I climbed aboard this beauty of a "passenger" ship, it was such a thrill to meet and greet so many of the over 400 missionary types, from over twenty (20) nations. I shall never forget the honor and privilege they accorded me by their invitation to be the Sunday service speaker. They were so gracious that when I stopped speaking they insisted that I continue. What a thrill to be standing in front of all those people from various nations – most of them serving without pay – because for them the main thing, was to keep the main thing the main thing! Keep thinking of others!

George and his wife Drena, who I met later, are a missionary team extraordinaire. Dale Rhoton and his wife Elaine, who I also met, are a perfect balance for George's perpetual motion. Dale is so cool and smooth, so you might say until you hear his impassioned speech. His wife Elaine is an accomplished author. George Verwer is a man that exudes unquenchable passion for world evangelism – his vision has no boundaries. I have to leave the O.M. story there. You can pick it up on the Web at O.M.Ships.com.

Bill Welte's mission (America's Keswick) is more local than international. America's Keswick is nestled in the sprawling pinelands of Whiting, New Jersey. To get a good take on Bill

– just think of the Renaissance Man! He is the C.E.O. of that amazing operation whose credo is – "where God speaks to hearts and transforms lives." America's Keswick was founded by Bill Raws who was a substance abuser and had a life transforming spiritual experience. A life changing-project for men in the shackles of addiction was launched over 100 years ago and is called the Colony of Mercy.

The Operation (or Ministry) of the Colony of Mercy is a Bible-based, compassionate system of recovery for men who seek help from God to deliver them from what they call "the monkey on their back." The men who became residents (3 months) come from all walks of life and bring with them some ugly and scary baggages – from armed robbery to – you name it! Would you believe that graduates of the program have returned to fill staff positions? Some have gone on to pastorates. There is even a member of the Board of Directors who is an alumnus of the Colony of Mercy! Can you believe that? I think this kind of history, past and current, is what energizes Bill Welte. To appreciate Bill is to see him in action. My impression of him, is that he has an incredible love for the people he refers to as residents of the Colony. America's Keswick provides year-round programs in a wide variety of church activity, including concerts featuring famous artists, pastors and church group retreats, family week vacations, youth camps, etc.

What is interesting about Bill is that he is personally in the front and center of all these activities. You can see that he enjoys every moment of it, because he loves his work with people. That's not the end of Bill – no question, when you see him leading song service, playing the piano, chairing the sessions, moving like a streak of light from one on-going event to the next – you wonder – how does he do all this? But wait, you may ask Bill, if you really want to know, ask him! You have to see him hug and embrace these Colony of Mercy residents, all of whom he knows personally. That's his real passion. Bill's thinking is about the miracle of God. It is literally a miracle how God actually speaks to the hearts of these men who come to the Colony almost drowning in a sea of hopelessness. Then in a few months by God's grace and the compassionate attention by the Colony of Mercy staff – these men can swim ashore and find firm footing not in the sinking sands on the beach of depression and despair, but on the SOLID ROCK OF A TRANSFORMED LIFE THROUGH FAITH IN JESUS CHRIST.

So let's say thanks again to all those people like George and Bill who were and are **thinkers of others** and what they can do to impact and influence the lives of needy people through the message of God's grace, His love and abundant mercy.

On the other hand, and on the other side of our threesided-coin is the reality of thinkers whose pre-occupation, and inclination make us want to erase their memory from our thoughts. If you wish, we can skip thinking about these darkminded thinkers of evil. Are you now saying – what Ralph Waldo Emerson once said: "I am not afraid to follow a path because of where it may lead." OK let's take the step along that path and talk only briefly about some other notorious thinkers.

CHAPTER II

THE DARK MINDED THINKERS

Their evil thoughts and deeds produced history's worst tragedies

heer up my friend! The world we live in today, depending on where you live, may seem to be overcrowded with bad people – those whose preoccupation is Thinking of what bad things they can do to others. You and I can be thankful that there are more people who think like Mother Teresa and Albert Schweitzer than those who think like Adolf Hitler and Joseph Stalin. We will come back to these two later.

A brief look back into the first record of man's inhumanity to man – result of his evil thinking – is inscribed in the pages of the well known Bible story of the brothers Cain and Abel. These were siblings whose parents were Adam and Eve. Cain's flaming anger was fueled by jealousy towards his brother because his brother Abel's offering to God was accepted and his was refused. This Bible narrative informed us of the first known cold-blooded murder in man's long history of MAN vs. MAN. That fragile but sustainable thread of evil has been woven into the fabric of <u>Man's Thinking</u> and consequently into his evil behavior. We should be aware that the survival of our civilization is a result of the Thinking of people who Think – BENEVOLENCE vs. Malevolence in other words these people think of how they can help vs. how they can hinder and/or hurt others. How they can restore vs. how they can destroy.

Speaking of destructive thinkers makes us think of the expression that says – every coin has two (2) sides. This is a good segue into the other side of man – his bad side.

As we are about to switch from talking about people who think good thoughts that they pursue toward good actions, we almost want to avoid talking about bad people who think bad thoughts that they pursue towards disastrous actions against their fellowmen.

The archives of history are bulging with blood-stained records of men (occasionally women) who come to or seize power and thought only to dominate their fellowmen and expand their territory and rule.

In recent memory, two evil men pop into my thoughts as examples of thinking bad thoughts and actively using their political power to wreak death and destruction upon millions of innocent people. I am fairly sure you are thinking (I see you nodding your head) of the same two evil men – Adolf Hitler and Joseph Stalin. The first – Adolf Hitler, as a German youth was sentenced to serve five (5) years in Landsberg Castle, Munich for his involvement in the 1923 infamous Beer Hall Putsch. During these years in prison Hitler (as most prisoners do) had lots of time to THINK. THINK he did. He also read widely. He claimed to have been influenced by reading Henry Ford's autobiography – My life and Work and also Ford's later book titled The International Jew in which Hitler stated Ford's claim that there was a Jewish conspiracy to take over the world. Hitler seems to have been awaiting this little key to unlock the evil compressed in his disorderly and deranged mind.

Hitler went on to think of the Jews as people vastly inferior to his so-called Aryan superior or master race. He also conceived of all other races as similarly inferior.

During his prison years Hitler wrote Mein Kampf (My Struggle). In this grotesque pile of German distorted words there were hideous and odious expressions of the THINKING of a contorted evil mind. He laid out his thoughts reflecting German racial superiority in every field of human endeavor. He advanced the idea of propaganda to deceive and control the masses. His core passion was to exterminate the Jews and to expand German territory by military conquest. This he felt would make German Hegemony a reality and bring the world to the feet of Germany, in humble respect. Well, the rest of the story is one of the most horrible narratives of man's inhumanity to man. The morbid self-destruction of this demon of evil thinking seemed too light a reprisal for this horrible thinker of evil deeds. The extermination of six (6) million Jews, including women and children, destroyed in the never-to-be-forgotten Holocaust of Auschwitz and Dachau will never be erased from the history of that dark, dismal and tragic period. No wonder the age old puzzling question – who made this man?

While all the genocidal madness was unfolding in Germany – over in Russia – the Soviet Union – there was the rise to political power of another tyrant Evil Thinker – his name, Joseph Stalin. Stalin (1878-1953) an avowed communist advanced to become Secretary the Communist Party and subsequently succeeded Vladimir Lenin as head and Dictator of the Soviet Union. His thinking was not the welfare of his fellowmen but about political power domination and economic rigor. His erratic and oppressive laws upset the agricultural system and was so severe that the Soviet System rapidly became a wasteland of famine – everything everywhere was rationed.

During the late 1930's Stalin launched – the Great Purge also referred to as the Great Terror. His thinking was that might makes right. He thought and executed every evil action the mind of an evil man could conceive including the Gulag Labor Camps where he imprisoned and banished millions of Russians and ethnic minorities. The story of his non-aggression pact with Germany and his collusion with his companion in evil – Adolf Hitler – is so chilling that it is best forgotten.

After World War II Stalin installed an oppressive communist regime in Eastern Europe that became known as the Eastern Bloc. Behind that bloc he hung what he called the Iron Curtain. Stalin then launched a cold war with a pledge to bring down the World System of Capitalism in submission to his system of World Communism.

As we look back at the notoriously tragic period of human sadness and suffering, we wonder aloud – what spurs the human being – Man – into the ugly and relentless pursuit of such savage contempt for his fellowman?

Joseph Stalin, like Adolf Hitler, died without even a glimpse of his ill-conceived fantasy of national glory. As we reluctantly look back at these demon-inspired thinkers of extreme evil – we expect no answers but we ask the questions anyway – **what were they thinking?**

While you are thinking up thoughts about the thinking of the people we briefly discussed and before we go to another well deserved rest break, do you recall – "The Man in a House by the Side of the Road?" His quandary or musing, you might say, becomes real in the conversation we are having about the actions of our fellowmen resulting from their Thinking. As he sat in the house by the side of the road, he saw so many men go by, some were good and some were bad – he kept thinking about good and bad men. We are even more puzzled because we have been discussing people like Mother Teresa, Albert Schweitzer vs. men like Adolf Hitler and Joseph Stalin et al. Remember that proverbial two sided coin and the two faces of the moon – ½ pearly white and shining while the other ½ totally dark? We have been puzzling over this mysterious duality in man – his apparent two (2) sides. What a puzzle is man! – in other words – what a mystery in his thinking about himself vs. his fellowman! It seems we keep bumping into this same conundrum of man. Why are we seeing two completely opposite streams flowing from the same fountain?

You know what – let's sit down under this tree, catch our breath and do a little relaxed thinking before we resume our stroll. What have you got up your sleeves? While you are grappling with your thoughts let me reach for the portable radio I tucked in my backpack along with my Bible – I don't leave home without them. Listen to this – breaking news-on the radio, coming out of Tucson, Arizona where a single shooter killed six (6) people including a nine (9) year old girl and wounded thirteen (13) others. The wounded included Congresswoman Gabrielle Giffords who is in critical condition from a bullet that passed through her brain. The details are so gruesome that they only bring back memories of so many – too many – far too many scenes of violent tragedies resulting from man's violent actions against his fellowman. The early reports say that the shooter – Jared Loughner had been thinking out this violent attack for 2-3 years. This murderous act against innocent people sprang from Jared's twisted thinking.

As I think of this non-stop violence occurring at all levels in our global society, including the African genocides and our current Afghanistan quagmire, I say thank God that the people who are thinkers of goodness, kindness, mercy, care, compassion and peace toward their fellowmen are far greater in number than those we discussed earlier that make us shudder just thinking of their ghastly deeds.

While we are relaxing during our break – you know what my question is don't you? That's exactly right! **What are you thinking?** Don't know why you are always want me to lead the way in our conversation. But I will always oblige just to lighten up the conversation during the break. Remember that expression I mentioned earlier about the two-sided coin? By the way, let's check it out! Do you have a coin handy? Ok – you've got a quarter. Don't give it to me – you just hold it in your hand so we can both get a creative look at it. This coin has this surface – we call (head) and we flip to the other surface we call (tail). So! Are we finished with our inspection of this two-sided coin? Well – just swipe your finger around the edge. As we both do this we find – a third surface or side. So we have just created a new saying or bromide. **"There is a third side to every coin."** This, by the way, is just for a little clever relief from our serious discussions on Thinking.

On a more serious note, that third side will help us illustrate a third dimension if you will – to the thinking habits of some of our fellowmen or "fellowpersons."

Who are these thinkers – not good not bad – just "free thinkers."

CHAPTER 12

A RARE BREED OF THINKERS

Their thinking defies all boundaries

These free thinkers see no boundaries. They display a rare pattern of intelligence. They are obsessed with finding answers to questions that are not even asked by us average mortals. Among them are people who consider themselves Pure Thinkers e.g., pure mathematicians, pure physicists, pure researchers. In other words they unwittingly apply an unusual level of intellectual curiosity and acumen in their quest for break-through and consequent contribution to our civilization. Without a doubt, their work continues to be invaluable to the world we live in here and now.

Again, who are these Free/Rare Breed of thinking persons? They are not the missionary-minded humanitarian and philanthropic type of thinkers. They are not those who imagine the most gruesome acts of violence that they inflict upon their defenseless fellow human beings. They are not in hot pursuit of scandalous wealth. Who are they? They emerge from all over planet earth. They all share a common trait – they are curious, creative and critical thinkers.

The truth be told, we owe a great debt of gratitude to these gifted marathon thinkers, who generation after generation, contributed so much to the convenience, comfort and well-being in the life we enjoy today. Science and Technology are advancing at so fast a clip that we take their amazing achievements for granted. Some of these thinkers revel in the sheer beauty and elegance of so-called "Pure Thinking." They have little concern about how and when the product of their thoughts could or should be applied. One of these "Blue-sky" thinkers was overheard saying: "May our elegant work have no useful purpose at all – never!" Can you imagine that kind of talk about that kind of thinking?

People like the early Greeks; Plato, Aristotle, Socrates, Aristarchus, Anaximander and other streams of thinkers like Copernicus, Brahe, Galileo, DaVinci, Newton, Euclid, Pascal, Madam Curie, Einstein, Hawking et al, These purist thinkers all deserve our admiring salute for all their monumental contributions to progressive thought. We should find a way to celebrate these and other trailblazing thinkers who for years and years before our generation spent most of their lives thinking imaginatively, ingeniously and insistently about the issues that challenge our physical existence and survival from day to day.

These are the thinking giants who never saw an obstacle that could not be overcome by their ingenious thinking. They never thought of darkness so dense that a glimmer of light could not dispel. In other words, they asked – why should we all fumble in the dark and fall asleep soon after the sun withholds its light? Why not – think of a way to make our own light shine – so that the darkness will submit to the light we invent or discover? Why not – think of a way to transmit sound – so that we are not limited by distance when we wish to hear or be heard? These are just for starters.

Let's kick around a couple more areas of our creative thinkers. You might say thinkers outside the box. These gifted thinkers were obsessed with thinking about challenges, issues, or situations that must, in their view, be brought into subjection by the creative mind of man. You know I was just thinking that it's such a disservice to the memory of these legendary benefactors of our postmodern world, to take so much of their work for granted.

I am sure that you must be thinking of a few other gifted thinkers and inventors. A few of those, in random areas, that come to mind: Euclid (Greek), and Archimedes (Greek/Italian), who were stars in a firmament all of their own making. Euclid (300 BC), thought out the concepts of measurements of various shapes and their multi-dimensional surfaces. Their complex relationships of angles and ratios are the tools we use everyday wherever we are – remember Geometry? – you hated it? What did you hate? Memorizing all those Theorems and working through the proofs? I thought it was real fun! So did Euclid! Isn't it strange that after over a half a century I still remember that base angles of an isosceles triangle are equal.

Archimedes was another legend of his time. It has been said and written that Archimedes was the world's first great scientist. He was first to approach scientific problems using what we call today the Scientific Method. "Give me a place to stand and I will move the earth," said Archimedes. No question about his confidence in his thinking gift. He went from thinking through one Mathematics problem to another. For example; the ratio of the circumference of a circle to its diameter π. This little Greek letter still remains the most puzzling ratio in mathematics presented to man on this planet. Can you keep a secret? I am working on it! This was a big focus of Archimedes. He next tackled the secret of why and how objects float in a fluid. On your next vacation cruise say thanks to

Archimedes. The physical principle of buoyancy bears his name as do many other ingenious inventions including the "Spiral of Archimedes" used in many types of pumping devices. People like Archimedes and Euclid were not only original thinkers – they were also free thinkers – they experimented with their thoughts and showed the world the results of their ingenious thinking. Thank you Archimedes!

It's safe to say that between the 18th and 21st Century there have been more spectacular breakthroughs in our modern world of Science and Technology than in all the centuries before in man's long history. There have also been so many brilliant thinkers who have astonished us with the ingenious depth of their thinking. A couple of random legends may lighten up our conversation and provide some respite from some of the heavy stuff that can cross our minds.

Did you ever stop to think of who or what was your greatest career motivator as you were growing up? Who sparked that CAN DO! MUST DO! Drive that made you want to aspire and achieve? You look a bit puzzled while you are puzzling through your thoughts – without thinking, I can tell you that my reading of Thomas Alva Edison's biography was a real igniter of my motivation and my determination to succeed. I said if only the good Lord preserved my health and well being I could live my dreams. As you can see, unworthy as I am – He did. He kept me all these years and He is doing that as we speak. Do you realize He is doing that for you also? Let's keep this conversation on track – back to Edison and this remarkable story of a young boy whose mother was called to the school he attended only to be told by his teacher that Thomas was beyond learning – he just could not cut it in any of his subjects. I can still see the picture of his mother Nancy, firmly holding his little hand while leading him away from school, but not before turning to his teacher to say these words, "The world may never hear about you, but it will certainly hear about my son." How about that? That is exactly why we are talking about Thomas Edison as one of those stalwarts in the pantheon of celebrated thinkers. Edison's hearing loss that handicapped his learning ability in his early school years did not impede his rapid consumption of information which he gained from endless reading.

Edison was constantly thinking, as he rolled out one patent after the other. He was constantly thinking: What do people want that he could invent to make life more comfortable and convenient? Finally, his most famous invention for which he is known world-wide and for which he will be always remembered – the incandescent light bulb. Someone has said: "Let there be light and there was Isaac Newton." I guess it can also be said, "Let there be Thomas Edison and there was light!" Edison could not stop thinking about people who wanted to be liberated from total dependence on the sunlight by day and who had to surrender to the darkness of night long before bedtime.

Edison the thinker and the consummate TINKERER was fond of saying: "Success is 99% perspiration and 1% inspiration." That 1% was inspirational thinking that lit up our WORLD. Thank you Thomas Edison!

Before we leave the campus of these stellar thinkers let's back up to our "Genius of Light" – Thomas Edison. Think a bit about his mom – listen to what she said: The world will hear about my son who his teacher has just pronounced a dunce – can't learn? Can you imagine the thoughts of that seven (7) year old boy as he heard his mother speak those inspiring words! What's your guess? My guess – he may have muttered under his breath – Go mom! We will show them! We will show the world!

I've got to digress and tell you this! I had a mother like that. I was as trouble-bug as any backwoods little boy could ever be – but my mother believed in me. She never told me so – she thought that was "bad psychology." How did I know that? I heard her many times when she thought I was not listening, saying to a neighbor, "He is as rude as they come, and sometimes I feel I could kill him, but he is very, very smart!" When I thought she would catch me listening, I'd run away pretending I did not hear. I did not become a Thomas Edison, but those words from my mother cancelled out all the hurt I felt from the severe punishment I received at her hands which I more than deserved. You know what– they were necessary to straighten out my crooked and distorted personality that she saw being formed in me.

Why did I bring this up about Thomas Edison's mother and my mother? Well – here is why? My mother impressed me as a lady who was not well educated but she was a <u>lady who was a thinker and a doer.</u> She whet my appetite for reading, and reading always triggered my thinking. Thanks mom! Perhaps that's why I read about Edison and his mom so vicariously.

I am making the same mistake we men almost always make – we don't give enough credit to the people who brought us into this world – <u>Our Women.</u>

CHAPTER 13

WHAT ABOUT WOMEN THINKERS

Do women think like men?

Do women think? You bet they do! Do they think like men? – I don't know that answer. You can read up on that subject in many books written on the subject or search the Internet. The point is, women have equal thinking capacity and they have demonstrated that fact over and over again.

While it's still fresh in your memory, think back on one of the most nail-biting, finger-crossing, breath-holding experiences in recent history. It has to be when the NASA Shuttle Columbia aimed its nose toward earth some time after a previous NASA ill-fated shuttle was completely destroyed in its abortive attempt to land in Houston, Texas. If you remember, no one survived that shuttle re-entry. Our private wish was that NASA would not repeat that mission. But they did! NASA planned a shuttle mission to deploy a highly sophisticated imaging device named CHANDRA. This device cost over 1.5 billion dollars and weighed about five (5) tons. For this mission they put a crack crew aboard that represented the best and the brightest astronauts. Who did NASA identify and assign to command this dangerous mission affording almost zero margins for error? It was U.S. Air Force Col. Eileen Collins. As you may recall she did a superb job as the whole nation waited to exhale. In Col. Collins' ascent to the highest height in NASA Shuttle program, she became the first woman to command a shuttle mission. In her assignment, she was responsible for all the technical aspects of the mission including the safety of her male top-of-the-line expert astronauts. All decisions and flight commands came from <u>Her THINKING!</u> At one point in the mission the computers for the shuttle's main engine malfunctioned. There was panic on earth. Not in the quick and sharp mind of Col. Collins. She thought her way through an acute and frightening emergency and successfully deployed CHANDRA in its functional orbit – to peer into the farthest reaches of space.

As we speak CHANDRA is scanning depths of intergalactic space not seen by the famed Hubble telescope. Her unusual skills and quick and accurate thinking did not escape the Russian Commander of the space station MIR. He radioed Col. Collins during the mission to say: "From the bottom of my heart <u>you are a courageous woman!</u>" He should have added – brilliant thinker with razor sharp mental reflexes. The Colonel's most severe test came in returning the shuttle safely to earth. Everyone remembered the shocking tragedy of the preceding NASA shuttle's return flight – regrettably no one survived! This Columbia shuttle's re-entry was of world-wide interest and many prayers were offered for their safe return. There was intense and anxious focus as we were all riveted watching our monitors with bated breath. So much depended on the integrity of the shuttle's heat shield to withstand the fierce thermal punishment imposed on the exposed surfaces. So, what was all this very high anxiety all about? It was about the fate of all these precious lives in the hands of a <u>lone female</u> in <u>sole command</u> of highly precarious maneuvers aboard one of the world's most advanced flying machines. While everyone was holding their breath at NASA and everywhere else, Col. Eileen Collins was calmly, cautiously, carefully, and precisely executing – that genius factor of the human mind – **Her thinking.** It almost feels like now we can all exhale and say – Bravo! Thank you Col. Eileen Collins! Next time you raise the question, as we did earlier, "can women think like men" – think Col. Collins. You may then say: maybe sometimes – sometimes they even out-think their male counterpart.

Now as we prepare to move on, let's stretch a bit and reflect a bit more. What are you thinking? Perhaps we should also ask what can we think? No hurry, we have a few miles ahead to cover in this **Thinking Wonderland.** Let's digest that last question – what can we think? We can think back to those brain-storming thoughts we've been kicking around and try to squeeze some conclusions from our discussions. Hold it! We can really try to answer the question – what and how we think about the mystery of man and his relations with his fellowmen?

CHAPTER 14

MANY PIECES OF
THE PUZZLE OF MAN

Looking at some of the mystery pieces

We are getting so very comfortable sitting here but we must move on before the sun goes down and we both get captured by the darkness of the night. I guess we'd just bed down among these beautiful trees and inhale the hypnotic aroma of the wonderland while the darkness of night punctuates our progress.

In the meantime can we briefly recap some excerpts of our spellbinding dialogue on the subject of the <u>mystery of man's duality </u>we could call it – the many <u>pieces to the puzzle of man.</u> Remember we reasoned that this duality came from his thinking. In the duality, we found as did the Poet Sam Walter Foss that there were some good men motivated by good thinking; there were bad men motivated by bad thinking. We observed that there were others who were just free or pure thinkers – the purely intellectual types – motivated only by their penchant toward curious exploration, inquiry and discovery. We discussed random examples of missionary types like – Mother Teresa and Albert

Schweitzer. These were people who constantly kept thinking about doing good things for others with no expectation of reward of any kind. We briefly considered Adolf Hitler and Joseph Stalin whose thinking was so gruesome that we would like to blot their names from our thoughts. Then there was the parade of geniuses – Super thinkers from Euclid, Archimedes, Newton, Edison, Einstein and more recently Stephen Hawking.

We did not even scratch the surface. In our repeated reference to "men" we both understood that this was generic and included females as well.

While Col. Eileen Collins took up the well deserved time in our conversation, there are other female thinkers of distinction who deserve our attention and gratitude for their contribution. Just to mention a random few: Everyone has heard of Madam Curie who in the 19th century discovered Radium and Plutonium and later isolated radium for a wide variety of uses including radiology for medical x-rays and other diagnoses. She became the first female Nobel Prize winner in Science.

Some other female super-thinkers who received Nobel Prize recognition are: Linda Buck for Olfactory Research (Biology). Albert Einstein said: Emmy (Amalie) Noether the first female mathematician elected to the National Academy of Sciences, was one of the most important Women Thinkers in the history of Mathematics. So we still did not find an answer to the elusive question – "Who made this THINKING man?" This man, this species – Homo sapiens – so multifaceted in his behavior, so ingenious in his thinking, so mysterious in his ways! I get the feeling that the Bible that I tucked in my back-pack for this trip is sitting there listening to our quandary and saying – "just open my pages again and find all the answers to your questions." You know that that's a stretch. Just my getting carried away about the Bible.

Let me show you a few verses that we have read before but perhaps will help to extend our thoughts regarding some answers to the Mystery of Man and perhaps another dimension of man beyond the mental machinery that makes him THINK. These verses will tell us clearly not only who made this mysterious creature but will give us insight into how, what, why, and where he fits into our UNIVERSE of created species. We may also find that God has great plans for him.

Did you notice that we really have to keep focused or we get distracted from this very important point of inquiry – Who made this thinking creature – man? Here, let's read together from my Bible. Let me find the verse that fits squarely into our quest. Back to Genesis to pick up our question. In Genesis Chapter 1, verse 26, here it says – you mind if we read it together again? *"And God said, let us make man in our image, after our likeness; and let them have dominion of the fish of the sea and over the fowl of the air (birds) and over the cattle, and <u>over all the earth,</u> and over every creeping thing, that creepeth upon the earth."* Now, verse 27 says: "So God created man in His own image, in the image of God created He them. And God blessed them and said unto them, be fruitful and multiply and replenish the earth, and subdue it; and have dominion over the fish and the birds of the air and every living thing that moves upon the earth." Now, these verses tell us why and what God did in creating man.

Another few verses will inform us where and how God did all this. By the way, despite my Science and Technology background, it is my view that the Holy Scriptures precede and transcend science. I have tons of logical reasons to accept the authenticity of the Bible's inspired record. I said I have tons of reasons for my rock solid faith in the Bible's reliability, how about you? Oh – that's funny you say you perhaps don't have many tons of reasons as I do you may just have one ton? Well I started with less than a fraction of a ton of faith in this Bible story – but that's another story – for later. Let's read on.

Now we read from selected verses that will show us further not only what and why of the creation of man, but later we will see that despite his very early slip and his historic fall – this unique creature man – has been and continues to be the primary and undeviating focus of God's attention, His favor, and His love.

Let's pick up our reading at chapter 2 verse 7 of Genesis. This says *"And the Lord God formed man of the dust of the ground, and breathed into his nostrils the breath of life; and man became a living soul."* This is a key point in our inquiry, remind me to come back to it later. Don't want to lose you in reading of these verses since I notice you look a bit distracted. I know we have read these verses earlier but be patient, you will see the reason for repeating some of them. So, here is the summary of events: The Lord God arranged a garden "Paradise" in Eden, and there He placed the man he created. The Lord then gave this man, Adam, specific instructions regarding his caretaking and landscaping work including his daily life sustaining provisions.

There was one caveat! There was a tree, called – **the tree of knowledge of good and evil** whose fruit was strictly forbidden for eating. The result of eating that specific fruit would be death (not physical), we will pick up this later. Lots to say on this point. The Lord said it was not good for the man, Adam, to be by himself, so he anesthetized him and removed a rib from his side from which he created a woman who he presented to Adam who called her – woman because she was taken from him, the man God had created. Chapter 3: 20 *"Adam called his wife's name Eve; because she* *was, in his eyes, the mother of all the living.*" Before we return to this dramatic point, which is before his expulsion from this garden paradise in Eden, let me fill in a gap between the verses we did not read but can return to later if you wish.

You remember, God gave clear and specific warning to Adam (not to Eve) that he should not eat of the fruit of the tree of the knowledge of good and evil? Eve fell for a deceptive influence and Adam was induced to disobey God's instructions. So we pick up the verse in chapter 3 and verse 22, "And the Lord God said, behold, the man is become as one of us, to know good and evil and now lest he put forth his hand and take also of the tree of life, and eat, and live forever." Therefore the Lord God sent him forth from the Garden of Eden to till the ground from which he was taken." Verse 24 says: "So he drove out the man; and he placed at the east of the Garden of Eden cherubim (angelic beings) and a flaming sword crossing in such a way as to prevent any attempted reentry by Adam and Eve." My friend, this was an unforgettable intersection in the very ancient drama of God and man! You ask why? Well, as we have read together – at this point God relegated the "Jewels" of his creation to a place we must call **the exit from paradise** (Eden). This God, we discussed earlier, who is omnipotent – can do anything. He could destroy Adam and Eve by the word of his mouth. He could create another couple with different restrictions – including restriction of their freedom. He could have set up an environment impervious to temptation and disruption of perfect harmony between God and his human creation. That is not what happened!

What happened at the exit of Eden? We read together the Bible record: God drove out the man and his partner – Adam and Eve were expelled! This could have been the end of an incomparably intriguing story. But, thankfully that was not the end.

CHAPTER 15

EXIT FROM PARADISE

The first paragraph in the greatest story ever told

The dramatic exit incident at the Garden of Eden, we discussed earlier, was not the end of God's relationship with his created masterpiece – the meticulous creature, He created after his own image. The expulsion of Adam and Eve from paradise, instead of being the end at the exit it became the lead paragraph in the <u>greatest story ever told</u> A story that continues to unfold.

No one can read Paradise Lost, the powerful literary saga by the 17th century poet John Milton, without being moved by its gripping, spellbinding drama. Milton, although totally blind when he wrote Paradise Lost, was not blind in recognizing that there existed a sovereign, omnipotent, omniscient, omnipresent God who was also graceful and gracious; merciful and loving. Milton excelled in his presentation of Paradise Lost as a literary masterpiece because he was thinking deeply about the same Bible Story we are sharing from the book of Genesis. In other words, when Adam and Eve left the Garden of Eden, they did not realize the omnipresence of their creator. They were unaware that they were equipped with technology that transcended any modern device conceived by the mind of man. They had no way of knowing, by self observation, that they were set up with a neuro-cardio system that could wirelessly transmit and receive information over the vast reaches of time and space and out perform any digital computer not yet designed. What is that technology you ask?

Ever heard of the human mind/human brain and by the way the human heart is a part of that technology. Let's hold this intrigue for later. We were saying that when God sent man out of the Garden of Eden, He set him up to be within hearing range of His voice and visual view of His eyes. In other words, God never let Adam and Eve out of His sight or out of range of His voice from the day he left the Garden exit. How do I know that? Give me a second or two to find a verse in the Bible that answers your question exactly. Is that in the Bible you ask? Well, here it is: 2 Chronicles chapter16, verse 9. "The eyes of the Lord run to and fro (back and forth) all over the world looking for those whose hearts turn toward Him." While we are at it, look at this verse at the other end of the Bible – In the book of Revelation chapter 4, verse 12. It reads: Let's read it together: "Thou art worthy, O Lord, to receive glory and honor and power, for You created all things, and for your pleasure they were created."

Wait a minute, this whole thing about man that got us so engaged is really about the mystery of his thinking. God's ingenuity was evident in His equipping man with thinking apparatus and communication apparatus so that He can always – speak to him and listen to him, and so that He can always see him and guide him. Wow! That's heavy stuff! Not really. You notice I stayed away from all that exciting discussion on cosmology and quantum physics. These among others are all particles of God's wonderful creation and can get us really excited. But let's not lose our focus. Where were we?

God sent Adam and Eve from the Garden of Eden – a paradise they lost – but God had a purpose and a plan for them and for all of us who share their gene pool. It's an amazing story that continues to unfold. What is truly amazing is that the key ingredient in the makeup of man is: His mind – **His ability to think.** His freedom to channel his thinking one way or the other. <u>Good</u> or <u>Bad!</u> But one more thing – we talked about earlier – His faith – man's Faith that allows him to believe. So can he be a thinker and a believer? He can be both in a logical sequence. I believe he thinks before he believes – Do you agree? Remember we talked about God wanting to have relationship with man – His creature. This by God's decree, requires faith. The Bible clearly states: without faith it is impossible to please God. That's why <u>the ingredient of faith will be at the core of our further conversation.</u>

We will take another break and be ready to sort out this very, very interesting thought about God's relationship with man. This should be very interesting and insightful.

You promised to hang with me all the way through this exciting trip in <u>thinking wonderland.</u> I took you at your word. We have only a few more miles to go before we part. Just in case, you for some reason, think of quitting now. Think this: There are a lot more miles to travel alone if you turn back. You will be alone with your thoughts. Think this also, the distance ahead is very short compared to the miles we have covered. If for some strange reason, none that I can think of, you decide to miss our discussion on The Greatest Story Ever Told, then think of what we learned at the "Exit at Paradise" – God has set you up to have a relationship with Him. Think about that! I am sure you will have some thought.

PART 3

WHAT ARE YOU THINKING ABOUT A RELATIONSHIP BETWEEN GOD & MAN?

IS THAT A POSSIBILITY?

CHAPTER 16

GOD'S RELATIONSHIP WITH MAN

The greatest story is still unfolding

Relationships! Relationships! Relationships! Why are we now thinking relationships? Lots of reasons not the least of which is the conversional relationship you and I struck up since we started this uncharted thinking adventure strolling through **Thinking Wonderland.**

We have been thinking discursively about a variety of things – amazing things! We have been thinking about a variety of people – amazing people! Transcending all of our mutual thoughts has been our thinking about the wonder of God. The Omnipotent God; the Omniscient God; the Omnipresent God! Let's not forget where we found the information source covering the greatest story ever told – The Holy Bible. The story is still unfolding because it is, you might say, timeless and fascinating. One of the key ingredients of that story is God and his relationship to man. This mind-bender will keep us on the edge of our seats and on the tip of our toes for the rest of the way.

This story is so mesmerizing that it eludes any human mind to grasp and forbids any human pen to write. So, where should we start? It always helps to do a brief recap. In other words, recalling snippets of where we have been in our thinking exchange while strolling along. We started talking, I mean thinking, about God not as a religious concept but as a "person" enshrouded in invisible mystery, but revealed in the marvelous display of nature we see every day as we open our eyes. We noticed how He revealed His incomparable attributes by the things we can clearly see, such as the vastness of space, the complexity of cosmic galaxies, the mystery and precision of the mathematical and physical laws that govern our universe assuring the maintenance of their function and motion. We also talked about the monumental event in antiquity when God created man. Wasn't that awesome?

We noticed, as we read from the Bible in the book of Genesis, that during the five (5) distinct creation periods there was a perfect sequential layout of the heavens and earth. There were birds flying, fish swimming, dogs barking, lions roaring, horses prancing, monkeys climbing, and all kinds of animated activity resulting from those periods of God's meticulous creation. There were also a diversity of flowers blooming, and trees bearing a delightful variety of fruits. There were also trees for shading the sun's rays as well as all manner of vegetation sprouting from virgin fertile soil in the cradle of creation. No wonder they later called that area – the Fertile Crescent. One more thing, on the sixth (day) of the creation period, God rolled out his masterpiece of creation.

This ingenious product, of the mind of an Omnipotent God was complete with "His image" stamped on and in him. Don't remember if we stressed this point in our repeated reference to the creation story and Garden of Eden, but God described this final act of creation as <u>Very Good!</u> You may want to check that out during our next break. (Gen. 1: 26-31)

CHAPTER 17

CREATED FOR RELATIONSHIP

We need a connection beyond ourselves

Perhaps at this point we should make our connection to the topic of Relationship with God, more focused and weave it into the fabric of all the thinking we have been sharing up to this point. Oh – wait a while! What's missing from this recap we have just skipped through? We said it would be a good precursor to that mind-tickling topic of relationship with God. In our recap, we are missing the part we discussed about man and his fellowman.

Remember we discussed this mysterious duality in man's behavior and curiously traced it to his disobedience to God's specific warning, to stay away from the tree of knowledge of good and evil. Although this actual tree (we believe) was symbolic of God's "faithfulness" (kept His promise), man disobeyed and became estranged from God and was penalized by being expelled or <u>disconnected</u> from God. In other words, although he did not literally physically die when he disobeyed those clear instructions – Adam and Eve (our forbears) were <u>disconnected</u> from God. That is another way of saying – God's relationship with His created beings was broken. But not beyond repair or renewal! Well, let's get more basic and more specific about the relationship factor. By way of definition: relationship is a connection between/ among things or people. I think this definition will stand the test of any issue popping up as we think through this interesting question of – can we have a relationship with God? You can kick around the converse if you will, i.e., can God have a relationship with us?

Let's face it, we have been in this thinking jamboree for quite a stretch of time covering a lot of miles of thought. We have had a lot of practice and enjoyed the mental experience. You are enjoying it you say? I am too! For this wind-up discussion about relationship with God we need to pull our thinking caps closer to our ears and remember that the key tools of our thoughts are – the questions we ask ourselves as we search for answers.

What are some questions for starters? Some questions pop into my mind, how about you? I am getting used to your asking me to go first. Again I'll oblige!

First question: why are we talking about relationship in the first place? Answer: you say we both benefit from the dialogue we have been having. Why? Great insights, no fights (smile). Our conversation has been just really eye-opening thinking. Really enjoyable, at times, especially when we thought about the good things done by good people that spring from good thoughts.

You know what – beyond ourselves there is a greater picture than ourselves because it includes all men – that is all men and women in our universe on planet earth.

So let me flush out some fundamentally interesting questions about God's relationship with man.

Before we get to the heart of relationship questions. I've got one quick one to pick your brain. Do you have a sense that most, if not all of us automatically and instinctively feel the need to make connection beyond ourselves. I mean, it's like a steady rippling stream trickling in the backwoods of our minds quietly almost hypnotizing us into thinking of a relationship beyond – romantic, beyond social, beyond economic, beyond religious, beyond political, beyond any machination of our making.

It seems at times that our deepest persistent need is that missing spiritual link. We struggle to find a paragraph or even a sentence in our thinking to properly describe our thoughts. Maybe just a single expression will simplify our thoughts. Do you agree that at some point in our living experience we seem to be quietly searching even probing mentally for that missing link? Could that missing link emerge as we continue our discussion? Could it be that the missing-link sense we feel, usually in quiet moments, is really a need for a connection – a relationship with God? I think for many of us, our thoughts about this mostly unexpressed but deeply felt relationship – a relationship beyond ourselves – goes way, way back in antiquity.

Remember our Bible reading in the Book of Job where this question was raised, "Cans't thou by searching find out God? Cans't thou find out the Almighty unto perfection?" Job wanted to make a connection – Job wanted to reach – with his sixth sense – to find out God – to connect with Him. He felt incomplete and perhaps insecure without this connection – this relationship he yearned to have. It's a kind of instinctive search of the heart and soul of man.

Much later after Job's time and closer to our time was a man whose life of piety and also his works of literature, left us these words about man's indomitable quest for a connection to God, "Our hearts are created for Thee O' God and they are restless until they rest on Thee." This was the expression that came from the thoughts of St. Augustine whose life was radically changed as a result of the connection he made with God. That's a very interesting story but we will not allow any diversion to our trend of thought about the question of the unspoken need that many of us feel for a relationship with God.

In further consideration of this critical link in our chain of thought about our relationship craving, let's think for a moment about the origin of this need we all feel, at some level of our consciousness. The need to be connected with God keeps popping up and never seems to quit – why is that?

CHAPTER 18

WE ARE PROGRAMMED FOR RELATIONSHIP

Inside all of us – a high tech wireless system

Let's stay with the question you just asked. Why do you feel this (almost) subconscious need for a God connection? Why is that? You cornered and stumped me for a moment. But a light came on in my thinking that I know will answer your question about why we human beings (mankind) feel the need for connection or relationship with God! Think back, think slowly, remember when we repeatedly read together from the Bible (Genesis) about those creative acts of God? Stay with me on this very critical point: In the act of creation God breathed in the man and man became a "living soul" which together with the breath of God included a wireless system enabling a two way communication connecting God and man.

Isn't this a SUPER genius God? Remember now, when this system was installed man was still within reach of the sound of God's voice. Why this pre-installation of a system so fast forward and ULTRA high tech? Well, you can see that God, who is

Omniscient, knew that our forbears – Adam and Eve would be expelled from His presence and that they and their offspring (you and me) would need this unique equipment to be connected and stay connected to Him – in other words, they were wirelessly equipped to communicate and be connected with God! Wow! Isn't that mind-boggling? This is exciting stuff! If we think this is a figment of our imagination, what about the buzz we just heard on radio and watched on the TV game show Jeopardy. The report is that an IBM team of hotshot scientists and engineers created a digital device named "Watson". Incidentally, "Watson" is named for IBM's founder – Thomas J. Watson whose credo for BIG BLUE was <u>THINK!</u> In the encasement of "Watson" are the products of all manner of technology breakthroughs. These super high-speed circuits handle algorithms (programmed commands) at near the speed of light, and in doing so they outpace (not outthink) man's reflexes and his responses.

To cut a long story short, after three (3) trips to the podium with two (2) of the top guns of Jeopardy fame – guess who won the contest? "Watson"!

Don't look so disappointed as if to think that man who was created originally by God was intellectually overpowered by a machine ("Watson") created by the BIG BLUE IBM "crack" team. <u>Not at all! Not at all! Not at all!</u> You see, "Watson" has these millions of responses or answers to every Jeopardy question pre-loaded in his database. When "Watson" receives the question translated into his cyber language – "Watson" at lightning speed goes searching for the best match to answer the question. Did you notice that although "Watson" won the Jeopardy contest he answered a question that placed a United States city in Canada?

So what's the point? Here is the point: God the Omnipotent, Omniscient, Creator embedded in the human being a system that allows not only super-fast thinking ("Watson" <u>cannot</u> think) but allows for endless questions and searching for answers. "Watson" cannot by "himself" raise a single question – no matter how simple. Not even the question of a babbling infant – constantly keeps asking; why mom? Why dad? This should not diminish our respect for the marvels of computer science as it explores Artificial Intelligence (A.I.). What an amazing insight we are gaining into the super ingenious God we have been thinking and talking about – are you ready for this? God has embedded in the Human Genome a <u>wireless</u> system that not only is unmatched in technical integrity to enable two-way communication but includes a spiritual software specific to every one of the 7 billion mortals on earth. How does that grab you?

So, wait a minute! Is that the spiritual software you had in mind when you were going on about the urge, the prompting, and the quest in the mind of man to be connected with God? That's right! God put it there! Says who? Says the Good Book – The Holy Bible! Remember Job 32:8, we read earlier where it says: "There is a spirit in man and the inspiration of the Almighty giveth him understanding?"

I think it's worth the time we took and the route we took to get an answer to the question: Do we feel a need for a relationship with God? Answer: We do, because God programmed this connection-urge in our spiritual DNA, and set up wireless antennas for two-way communications! Why? So He can relate to us and we can relate to Him.

We did the best we could to address the question: <u>Do we feel a need</u> for God? And talked a bit about why we (most of us) have this sense of reaching beyond ourselves to connect with some "entity" greater than ourselves. In other words with some intangible sixth sense we keep reaching upwards for connection, because deep inside the reaches of our souls – we feel disconnected – we yearn and privately keep reaching (unconsciously sometimes) for a relationship with God.

As we move right along we must ask another and perhaps even more searching question. <u>Is it Possible To Have A Relationship With God?</u> The answer may seem obvious based on our prior exchange of thoughts about how God has ingeniously programmed man for relationship with Himself, but we must not shortchange our thinking about this possibility. Before we put "Watson" (the wiz computer) behind us as we move forward in our conversation, a few words of acknowledgement are in order for the creative scientists and engineering teams that produced this digital wiz. Their work is an example of our repeated insights regarding the intellectual gifts with which men are endowed by God.

Realistically, "Watson" is, at best, a digital gofer and his/ its possibilities are limited because his/its creators are, like us, limited human beings. "Watson" receives digital signals/orders, then he/it goes rapidly to find matching answers to questions fed into the system. Is it possible for "Watson" to have one intelligent "emotional" exchange with another "Watson"? – e.g., "I am sorry we don't think like those gifted humans who created us" No! Absolutely No! "Watson" has no feeling – he/it has none of the five (5) human senses. Does "Watson" have a feeling of need for a relationship with God? You answer that one! There goes the story of man and the machine he created.

CHAPTER 19

EXAMPLES OF HISTORY – BEGIN WITH BABEL

Relationship between God and man
is that a possibility?

Our question now will focus on the possibility of God's Relationship with man. I have become accustomed to your laconic responses – just a very few words, but I can see you are doing a lot of silent thinking on the question of the possibility of God's relationship with man. The truth be told I have a difficult time handling that as a concept intellectually. I just thought of the best idea ever – why not go back to our information source, not for intellectual help but for historic events described in the Holy Bible. Before we come back to the Bible for some illustrative examples of this God/man relationship possibility a thought just crossed my mind that may seem irrelevant but not really. Remember Andrew Carnegie's sound bite that says, that The Business of America is Business? That in part is due to our excellent American Business Education System. Most of the premier Graduate Business Schools in America employ a teaching tool called the Case Study Method.

In order to demonstrate the realities of business management, the professors/instructors actually bring to class "real life" information about business performance – the good and the bad. How profits are made and lost. How people are hired and why some should be fired. They expose students to concepts of business analysis but they take them beyond possibility studies by use of a very successful teaching model called – The Case Study.

The Bible provides us with case studies that fit squarely into all situations that man has not even yet imagined. A few case studies, to illustrate the answer to our question – Is it possible for God to have relationship with man and conversely man with God, will help us far better that trying to get answers by intuitive inferences.

My first thought is the case of Babel. In the Bible book of Genesis (chapter 11:1-9) there is an intriguing part of the story of man's development. The passage reads:

"Now the whole world had one language and a common speech. As people moved eastward, they found a plain in Shinar and settled there. They said to each other, "Come, let's make bricks and bake them thoroughly." They used brick instead of stone, and tar for mortar. Then they said, "Come, let us build ourselves a city, with a tower that reaches to the heavens, so that we may make a name for ourselves; otherwise we will be scattered over the face of the whole earth." But the LORD came down to see the city and the tower the people were building. The LORD said, "If as one people speaking the same language they have begun to do this, then nothing they plan to do will be impossible for them. Come, let us go down and confuse their language so they will not understand each other." So the LORD scattered them from there over all the earth, and they stopped building the city. That is why it was called Babel—because there the LORD confused the language of the whole world. From there the LORD scattered them over the face of the whole earth." Keep remembering that man is a thinker. He is an explorer.

He is an innovator. He has the superior benefit of language – a means of understandable communication. The passage we just looked at together captures these distinctives of man. It also tells us that this band of men was bent on seeking fame for urban organization and architectural break-through. The passage tells us that they were sort of nomads – but really smart – and they were communicating their thoughts and ideas about settling down (in the Fertile Crescent) in an area near Babylon (Iraq). This was a location that they could turn into a dream world. Please don't ask me why I am breaking out into this broad smile. Have you seen the fantasy-like pictures of the ultra-modern skyscrapers (reaching up to Heaven) being constructed in Dubai? This is a Muslim city where they are determined to make a world-renowned name for themselves without any or very little acknowledgement of God or any priority on any relationship with God. Fact is – it's a showcase of the fantasies that money can create if you have enough of it. It is also a showcase of sensual and erotic fantasies that the mind of man can think up when he avoids response to God who is reaching out to him for a relationship – nothing new is there?

As we speak, this construction is taking place in the dream world of Dubai. It tells us something about our species when we read from the Bible and notice that these events around the Tower of Babel are pretty much a xerox copy of the Dubai extravaganza to memorialize the genius of man. So much for Dubai – not very far from Shinar the site of the Tower of Babel. On that bit of digression you seem so surprised and thoughtful as you listened.

Let's return now to our story of man, playing out at Babel, in the early stages of his development. We also begin to see some interesting inclinations in his behavior. As these people were traveling, perhaps, thousands of them. They were not like our notorious Republicans and Democrats fighting always – they were pretty united. They must have had a leader don't you think? They were all speaking the same language. You say – it must have been English? Could be. The Bible doesn't tell us that. It just says they were all speaking the same one and only language.

They also had the instinctive smarts (remember we discussed that earlier) to use raw material found in their environment (the Fertile Crescent) in Mesopotamia to make bricks and mortar. Their thinking obviously was – "if we can invent materials for construction – we can construct anything! Let's start with a City Planning Committee that will come up with a plan to lay out a-knock-your-socks off urban spectacular. By the way, for all this genius we are discovering among ourselves – we don't really need the God that our ancestors talked so much about."

They may have also thought further, let us pull together a Tower Committee. They will be charged with coming up with plans and specifications for a tower not to be out-done by any generation following us. When this tower is built – we want our name engraved all over it. And another thing they kept, perhaps, remembering God's original statement, passed on by their ancestors, that His purpose of creating Adam and Eve is that they should not only multiply but that they should spread out all over the face of the created habitable space on planet earth. What do you know? This bunch of "smart alexes" would have none of that kind of thinking.

What were they thinking? What do you think – you don't know? Well here is what I think that they were thinking! "We are smart enough to come up with ideas about a city where we can park and not have to live like nomads. We are smart enough to invent materials of construction using the raw material of the soil under our feet. We are smart enough to organize groups of thinkers who can conceive objectives and set up tasks leveraging the concept of division of labor. We can include in our objectives something that will blow your mind. Listen to this – no disrespect – but we do not need God to help us think. We feel sometimes when we are really quiet and relaxed that God is out there somewhere and maybe within us there is a connection we need to make but then again, the reality of our smart thinking just washes all that God thinking away as the waves wash the sands up on the sea shore."

"The bottom line is – with our native smarts, we have a vision of an exciting urban model really modern. None like it built before and most likely none can be its equal for a long, long time to come. More importantly we will live right here in Shinar (Babylon). Our name will be stamped on this wonder of the world. There is one last thing – we need a committee to ensure that our name and fame spread worldwide. And another thing, if by chance there are other beings like ourselves who hear about us and visit with us to see the miracle of our urban showcase and the breathtaking spectacle of our Tower of Babel reaching up to heaven – let them come to visit! Before they arrive, they must be informed that our language is the one and only language spoken here. If they can't and won't learn our language – don't come!" While the Bible text does not present that level of detail we are pretty much in the ballpark of the thinking of the people of Babel based on what they said (Genesis 11:3-4)

This is what they said to each other, "Come let us make bricks and bake them thoroughly – come let us build ourselves a city, with a tower that reaches up to the heavens, so we may make a name for ourselves and not be scattered over the face of the whole earth."

This is our first "case study" illustration of man's relationship with God gone awry because of their collective bent on doing their own thing with concerted effort to leave God out of their thinking – at least on that occasion.

But wait. how do we see God in the picture here? Well, the next verse in Genesis chapter 11:5 says it all. It reads:

"But the Lord came down to see the city and the tower that the men were building," The Lord said, if as one people speaking the same language, they have begun to do this, then nothing they plan to do will be impossible for them. Come let us go down and confuse their language so they will not understand each other."

So the Bible text continued to read that God used the confusion of language to stop the monstrosity of the tower that was sure to come crashing down as they pushed further and further upward. And so the name Babel was attached to that event in history because of the language confusion and the dispersion of the people to various parts of our planet.

What does our case study show? If we look together, we will see God the creator, whose eyes move back and forth over the whole earth keeping track of his creation/people. We see that, despite their we-can-do-it-without-God thinking and actions – God expressed not only a passing interest in what they were doing but reached out to connect or have a relationship with them by what He did. What did God do? He saved a small population of people from the sure tragedy that would result if they continued to push that tower upwards given their limited skills in structural architecture and building. God wanted those people spared for a cherished relationship with Him! My next case study illustration of the possibility of God relating to man will pick up on the demographics of these same people who spoke one language and whose progeny now are located in various geographical areas near the cradle of creation – the Fertile Crescent – we call it in our time.

By the way did you catch the point that God intervened not only to disrupt the urban planning and tower construction, but did you see that God's purpose was to make His presence felt as the Omnipotent one without whom they could do nothing. This loving and caring God reached out to them and activated their God-man relationship software installed at the creation event we discussed earlier. So then QED as we say in Mathematics – it is God who makes it possible for His created beings and their offspring to have a relationship with Him!

CHAPTER 20

GOD'S RELATIONSHIP
WITH ABRAHAM

Abraham – A legend of his time and our time

Where do you think we should go for our next Case Study of God's relationship with man? Looks like you are still digesting that historical event at Babel where our early ancestors made an organized and intrepid attempt to show that they were so smart and skilful that they could do whatever their minds conceived without any help from God!

If you need a few minutes to think further about that Babel fiasco – I'll wait for your signal, so we can move on to our next Case Study. We can think of this case of God reaching out to a man by referring to God's discovering and recruiting Abraham. Abraham you say? I can understand if you think I am thinking of the 16th President of the United States – Abraham Lincoln. I can see why you would think of this towering figure in American History, especially since there is a current nationwide observance of the 150th Anniversary of the Civil War. This was an event that threatened to rip apart the loosely woven fabric of the United

States, leaving scattered threads of disunity bearing labels marked: North and South!

This was a time that called out for the nation's president, the leader of a democratic republic, still in its infancy, to shine and lead the nation out of the darkest period of its history.

There are a lot of books written, documentaries made, stories told about this period in the mid 19th century America. There are a lot of views offered regarding Abraham Lincoln's deeds, his decisions and his motives for those decisions. By all accounts, they were in the interest of saving the Union of the United State of America. The fierce and ugly battle among citizens of our beloved land, where so much blood was shed and so many lives were lost is a sad and somber memory. Why do we remember Abraham Lincoln in his role as the nation's leader? Because he was unquestionably the chief mitigator of that long and bloody struggle.

The remarkable thing about Abraham Lincoln in my view, was his sensitivity to the supremacy of the Role of God in the governance of the Nation. In his second inaugural address referring to the North and the South he said: "Both read the same Bible, and pray to the same God; and each invokes his aid against the other. — the prayers of both could not be answered – that of neither has been answered fully." He went on to wrap up his inaugural address by saying: "Fondly do we hope – fervently do we pray – that this mighty scourge of war may speedily pass away. Yet, if God wills that it continue until all of the wealth piled by the bondman's two hundred and fifty years of unrequited toil shall be sunk, and until every drop of blood drawn with the sword, as was said three thousand years ago, so still it must be said: the judgments of the Lord are true and righteous altogether. With malice toward none; with charity for all; with firmness in the right, as God gives us to see the right, let us strive on to finish the work we are in; to bind up the nation's wounds; to care for him who shall have borne the battle, and for his widow, and his orphan – to do all which may achieve and cherish a just and lasting peace among ourselves, and with all nations."

How can we ever forget the president's history-making speech delivered at Gettysburg, PA. where he stated that: "Four score and seven years ago our fathers brought forth on this continent a new nation, conceived in liberty and dedicated to the proposition that all men are created equal. We have come to dedicate a portion of that field as a final resting place for those who here gave their lives that this nation might live. It is altogether fitting and proper that we should do this." He concluded with these memorable moving words; "That from these honored dead we take increased devotion to that cause for which they gave their last full measure of devotion; that we here highly resolve that these dead shall not have died in vain; that this nation, under God, shall have a new birth of freedom; and that government of the people, by the people, for the people, shall not perish from the earth."

It should not surprise anyone if Abraham Lincoln's parents named him after the Abraham in the Bible. They may have seen or projected for him the characteristics of a boy who was determined to be a great leader and that the signature of his greatness would derive from his faith in God and his relationship with God. Our brief diversion was a fond reflection of an American Abraham who seemed called of God to lead our nation through one of its most tragic moments in our history. Thank you Mr. President!

As legendary a figure as Abraham Lincoln was in American History, he does not qualify for the case study we are about to consider. Abraham of Bible times will give us a rare insight into the reality of God's reaching out for a relationship with man –

and specifically identifying an individual as a <u>starting point</u> of His plan. Where do we start and what is the point? First a direct answer to the questions and then we can think through some very, very interesting and very surprising details.

Where do we start? No surprise that we keep going back to the Good Book for our source information – so that's where we will start. What is the point? The point is that despite man's history of a getting-along-without Godattitude, God is always reaching out to have a loving relationship with man.

As I reach again into my backpack for my ever present Bible, to share some verses with you, I should explain the broad smile on my face. I was thinking of the American Express commercial about that credit card: "Don't leave home without it" I'll tell you, I have sometimes left home without my Amex card – but never have I left home without my Bible. You ask what about when you are driving along. You will always find a Bible on the passenger seat or glove compartment in any car I am driving. That's why we have the convenience of this copy in my backpack as we travel along in **Thinking Wonderland.**

CHAPTER 21

ABRAHAM THE FATHER OF NATIONS

Total faith in a voice never heard before

Let's look together in Genesis Chapter 12. Did you notice the connection? We have just finished reading about the Babel Event where God disrupted the attempt, by some of our early ancestors, to show that they did not need God because they were smart enough to do anything all by themselves. These same people spread out during decades of time and thousands of acres of fertile land watered by ever flowing rivers and rippling streams and refreshed by springs of unpolluted water. Did they learn some lessons from the Babel experience of their ancestors? A history of their idolatrous living shows that they did not. Did God give up on them?

The verses we will read together shows He did not. So here, let's read a few verses of chapter 12 to get started. It says: **"The Lord said to Abraham, leave your country, your people and your father's house and go to a land that I will show you. I will make you into a great nation and I will bless you. I will make your name great and you will be a blessing. I will bless those who**

bless you; and whoever curses you I will curse; and all peoples on the earth will be blessed through you." We could stop here but let's read a few more verses so we can really get into the case of Abraham. Here we read: "So Abraham left, as the Lord had told him; and Lot went with him. Abraham was 75 years old when he set out from Haran. He took his wife Sarai, nephew Lot, and all the possessions they had accumulated and the people they had acquired in Haran, and they set out for the Land of Canaan, and they arrived there. Abraham travelled through the land as far as the site of the great tree of Moreh at Shechem. All that time the Canaanites were in the land. The Lord appeared to Abraham and said: **"To your offspring I will give this land." So he built an altar there to the Lord, who appeared to him there."** No offence but I understand if these are more Bible verses than you read at any one time. At one time, I did not want to read any verses at all. But as we say at the B-School – let's "set up" this next case:

Here is a 75 year old man and his wife – a childless couple. They have some close relatives – uncle, nephew and others. They live among a population of thousands of people many of whom speak different languages and whose religious life centers around idol worship. You have heard the expression: "Looking for a needle in a haystack." Finding Abraham's residence among these thousands of multi-lingual people was pretty much like finding a needle in a haystack!

A few thoughts come to mind. Why would God want to find Abraham? How did He find him? Let's start with the second question first. You remember earlier in our conversation we had a fairly lengthy discussion on the big Three **O**'s that characterized God. One of them was His **O**mniscience: This means, He knows everything, sees everything, nothing is hidden from Him even in the darkest night or in the deepest secret thought of the minds of mankind. Because of this **O**mniscient factor, unique to God alone, He was able to know where to find Abraham at home. Look at the two sides of this interesting initiative. God on the one hand knew exactly where to find Abraham. He knew his temperament

of FAITH and his readiness to listen to a voice he had never heard before, and knew that he would follow his instructions to pack up and start a journey to "no-where" without a road map.

On the other hand, Abraham was faced with the unusual and unsettling situation of a sudden disruption of his peaceful, comfortable family life. He had no advance notice of this sudden change of his location and lifestyle. He never heard such a thing as a voice from God speaking directly to any member of his family or anyone else in the neighborhood. He was instructed to: "Get Out!" Not please leave if you can or when you can. He did not have a road map or GPS device to guide him on this mysterious journey. All he heard was: "I will show you where to go." That really was his equivalent to our modern GPS digital gadgets.

I remain amazed at how Abraham responded promptly, submissively, and courageously, and even more impressive was his TRUST OR FAITH in God of whom he know very little or nothing! Do you begin to get the picture? The picture sketched in our reading of Genesis chapter 12 forms the basis of our thinking about the case of Abraham as an illustration of <u>God reaching out to man for a relationship with Him.</u>

May I share with you a few thoughts on the passage we read together in Genesis chapter 12. This passage is widely referred to as "the Call of Abraham." I think of it as the call of God to Abraham. That's a semantic point! The real point is: <u>God does not work without a plan. He plans His work and then He works His</u>

plan. While we are at it let's give some support to that sound bite. Remember our earlier trips to the Book of Genesis. Every single step in the creation of the universe, from the very first verse, there was evidence of a precise, discrete and meticulous plan. This was evident day by day up to the sixth day that culminated in the creation of a living being – ADAM!

By the way, as a side bar comment, did you know that the ontogenetic experts as well as a variety of other scientific disciplines have confirmed that the sequential order of creation is, by the most advanced methods of scientific investigation, precisely accurate? Simple minded as I am, I did not need their confirmation I simply believed the Bible! How about you? Don't answer if you prefer. Where is our point? The point is that God's precision thinking is evidenced in the words of His mouth and the work of His hands.

So are you asking what has all this science verification stuff have to do with the call of Abraham? Well what do you know? See if you can connect with this. Before there was a knock on Abraham's door in the neighborhood of Ur of the Chaldees (near Iraq), God had a precise plan specifically for Abraham to Birth a Nation! The birth of a Nation! What is the basis for a statement so far reaching that includes a Nation? In a minute I'll answer that but not before I offer an appendix: Not only was God's plan to include a Nation, but it extended to all the nations of the earth! Where did I get that Information? Look at verses 2 and 3 of Genesis 12: Let's read again together: "I will make of thee a Great Nation, and I will bless thee, and make thy name great; and thou shall be a blessing, and I will bless them that bless thee, and curse them that curse thee; and in thee shall all the families of the earth be blessed.

You will see later as this exciting picture of God's plan unfolds, that God's plan in calling Abraham extended beyond Abraham, beyond the nation he would birth, and will culminate in a dramatic unfolding of His plan for all people of all nations. His plan is designed for all people everywhere to have a personal relationship with Him, and He with them. Abraham was a pivotal point in this master plan. You may find a few highlights from Abraham's epic adventure interesting and even surprising as we progress when you think that God could, by some means of His choice, prepare an extraordinary person and alert him regarding adventure he would make into strange territory. He could give him all the advance details he would need to be comfortable with such a radical shift in his personal life. So does it not surprise you that God chose a person just like both of us to undertake such an historic assignment?

No one should hesitate to credit Abraham for his faith and trust in God. The record shows that he was at the top of his game in this area of submission to God, devotion to God, believing in God and never questioning His plan. By the way, you notice I call him Abraham while the Scripture passage that first states his name calls him Abram. At one point in his colorful life, at 90 years of age God changed his name from Abram to Abraham meaning father of a great nation.

An important part of the brief highlights on Abraham's life is that when God called him to pack up and leave his family behind he gave him some specific and repeated promises. Let's take a look at what God told him. Keep in mind that in the plan of God – this is not just a favorite person selected to accomplish an extraordinary task. This is about God's relationship with people like you and me. Think of this, when Abraham left home he could only take so much of his material possessions on this journey and by the way – he was not coming back home ever! I notice that God did not provide him with spending money to keep him and his family whole (smile). So what did God give to Abraham as his farewell gift and guarantee for the mysterious journey?

CHAPTER 22

PROMISES, PROMISES, PROMISES

Abraham Is Loaded With Promises

Abraham received a bundle of carefully packaged Promises. Yes – Promises! Promises! Promises! You know the Bible is in a class by itself. There is nothing you and I or anyone else can think of that the Bible doesn't beat us to it or to put it another way – before we think a thought– the Bible has already addressed it – Isn't that amazing? So what about Promises we just mentioned – those were Abraham's only guarantee for the adventure ahead. So what does the Bible have to say about Promises that God makes? It says that <u>He does not fail one word of His</u> great promises. I think that's found in (1 Kings 8:56) you can check that out.

Now let's see – what did God specifically promise Abraham as he was packing his belongings to leave his native land of Ur, taking with him his wife, Lot and some ranch – herdsman? As we consider together, these Promises of God to Abraham, we must never forget that these promises are based on God's plan for His relationship with man. Does that quizzical smile on your face mean you get it? Ok! We are on the same page. Now, let's think a bit about the Promises – The first one: I will make <u>you</u>

a great Nation and I will bless you. The next: I will make your name great and you will be a blessing; I will bless those who bless you and curse them who curse you; and last: all the peoples of the earth will be blessed through you! Wow! What a package of Promises, Promises, Promises!

Would you be surprised that if you traced the winding path of Abraham's adventure that you would find that every promise that God gave to him was fulfilled? The Bible, as well as history, has shown that this patriarch, as he became known, accumulated great wealth, although he chose the life of a nomad living in temporary tents because he had a vision of the permanence of a heavenly city. From Abraham descended a great nation and more precisely – two nations.Are you aware of this part of the patriarch's life? It's both fascinating and timeless, because the consequence of his ill-advised action is making the news headlines even as we speak. If you think I am referring to the ongoing conflict in the Arab world and the never-ending hostilities between the Arabs and the Jews, you are right on target.

Listen to this. In addition to the general and sweeping promises that we read together from Genesis chapter 12. God further and specifically promised Abraham, that despite his age (about 100 years) and his wife's age (90 years) they would have a son to kick off the fatherhood of this nation that was stated in <u>the very first sentence of the promise.</u> Now listen closely! First, what does Abraham think? He may have been thinking like this: "Well God called me and gave me these promises when I was 75 years old. I have patiently waited for this miracle of old-age fertility to happen. My wife Sarah has also waited and every year since we received the promise she thinks – It may be this year we have this son of promise – our heir, <u>our first born.</u>" Abraham further thinks – Sarah is full of ideas. She has the idea about using their

Egyptian maid to help in fulfilling God's promise. We have waited these almost 25 years. Have you heard this story before? No? Or Yes? Both you say. Well Abraham concedes to Sarah's impatient reasoning and Abraham is now the father of a son named Ishmael, who to this infertile couple, was born to them first. Ishmael who was <u>born first</u> in the family of Abraham and Sarah was <u>NOT THE FIRST BORN PROMISED BY GOD.</u>

This is not a semantic point! This is a critical point. Are you aware that Isaac who was born following the birth of Ishmael, became the first generation ancestor of the Jewish nation? Are you also aware that Ishmael who was born first became the first generation ancestor of the Arab nation? I hope you share my excitement in seeing how God plans His work and works His plan. Did you notice that despite the apparent disruption in the plan for Isaac to be the first born to Abraham and Sarah his wife, the nation that came through the lineage of Isaac – The Jewish Nation remains the greatest wonder of the world of nations? For example: historically the Jewish nation has been a numerical minority compared to their repeated antagonists. Despite this handicap of size and military strength, miraculously the Jews have prevailed and survived. They even survived ancient and modern attempts to completely annihilate them. Why was such a small group of people occupying such a small slice of real estate in the Middle East so resilient and so invincible against all odds? By the way, their contributions to all areas of human endeavor have been astounding. Why is this? Remember these Promises, Promises, Promises we briefly discussed earlier?

The Jewish nation emerged descended from Father Abraham; wherever they settled they were blessed materially. Do you realize that in that package of promises that God gave to Abraham there was the one you might say was cryptic. I mention cryptic because

I don't think Abraham understood what was meant by: —— "all peoples of the earth would be blessed through you." In a much larger sense God was saying to him – down through your offspring via your FIRST BORN Isaac – I will display to all the world my ultimate plan and purpose: that is to have a personal relationship with every and all who will receive the message that this direct descendant of Abraham will bring and deliver to all the world. And who is this person prophetically encrypted in that promise – "all people will be blessed through you?" I am sure you will be surprised when we read together the clear and concise answer to that question in the passage which will kick off our final case study illustrating the unfolding story of God's reaching out to have a personal relationship with all mankind. Wasn't this case of Abraham exciting? Stay tuned. There is more to keep you engaged!

CHAPTER 23

THE ULTIMATE PROMISE FULFILLED

A personal blessing promised
to all nations of people

Our ongoing conversation strolling through **Thinking Wonderland** has brought us along the path of an astounding trajectory of events. These events include historical landmarks like the rise and fall of the most powerful and flourished empires that ever emerged. We also got various insights into their self-proclaimed rulers, some of whom called for the compulsory worship of their dominated and powerless subjects.

During all these tumultuous periods of power grabbing and nation-building, the Bible captures seminal points in time which showed that God repeatedly extended an endearing outreach for <u>personal</u> relationship with mankind. In our conversation case study we discussed the case of Babel which exemplified our very early ancestors showing off their independence from God and the fiasco that resulted. In the case of Abraham, into which we just really took a brief peek, we were captivated by Abraham's dramatic call that yanked him from his native neighborhood and took him on an epic journey where he experienced the reward for his childlike faith. That is he saw that every single promise that God made to him was guaranteed and was completely fulfilled – except one. Let's pick up on that trajectory of events and fast forward to where we left off in the New Testament section of our Bible. Would you be surprised about what we may find? Get ready for this, and keep in mind that this part of our conversation is focused on God seeking a personal relationship with mankind everywhere – all nations – all languages!

You are asking what about that one promise to Abraham I mentioned that was not fulfilled? Here, let's read together from the first book of the New Testament and the very first verse. It says here: " **The book of the generation of Jesus Christ, the son of David the son of Abraham.**" Before we go any further, now for the answer to your question about that one unfulfilled promise that God made to Abraham. Remember these words: **"And in thee shall all the peoples of the earth be blessed?"** Where is the connection you ask? The verse we just read together from Matthew's Gospel chapter 1 and verse 1 is a graphic display of a trajectory of history that started from that knock on Abraham's door alerting him to an abrupt and sudden change in his life. Also in this drama we see his response with childlike obedience to the voice of an invisible stranger.

This is the speed-oflight fast forward that brought us to the one verse that says it all. It says that the one unfulfilled promise to Abraham, which he most probably did not translate, was now fulfilled before our eyes and guess what? It's so spectacular, it's so mind-stretching, it's so heartwarming, and it's so soul-thrilling that it deserves to be given some unhurried slot in our continued conversations. Looks like we are coming up on our final break. It's been awhile since we have been making our way through the forestry of thinking. As we relax for awhile and digest these amazing thoughts we will be ready to take a second look at that verse that tells us what the whole New Testament Gospel is all about.

Tempus Fugit! Time sure flies when we are thinking and talking about such a variety of amazing things, people and events. Let's resume where we left off talking about that first New Testament verse in Matthew's Gospel. It presents Jesus Christ as the son of David and the son of Abraham. You think we have been dazzled by these events we have been covering during our conversation stroll in **Thinking Wonderland?**

I promise you, you will be mesmerized when I share with you some insights of information about that person introduced as Jesus Christ in the first paragraph of New Testament Scripture. Incidentally, I made up a "commandment" of my own, I call it the eleventh commandment. "THOU SHALT NOT ASSUME ANYTHING." I will not assume that you are aware who Jesus is or where he fits into God's plan in His outreach to bring us into a personal relationship with Himself. With that in mind let me ask your patience as I raise a stream of questions that you can give me answers to as you wish. Did you know that long after Abraham's time God directed many prophets whose messages clarified the ultimate promise made to Abraham that we discussed earlier? That's right! Some of these prophesies required close scrutiny to understand their meaning. Many others were very clear and unmistakably related to this promised unique person known in Hebrew Scripture as The Messiah.

For example, here are a few prophetic scriptures from the ever famous prophet Isaiah regarding the Messiah's birth: Look at this verse in the Old Testament (Isaiah 7:14) **"Therefore the Lord himself will give you a sign: The virgin will be with child and will give birth to a son, and will call him Immanuel."** The next two predicting the Messiah's birth are: (Isaiah 9:6) – **"For unto us a child is born, to us a son is given, and the government will be upon his shoulders and he will be called wonderful, mighty God, everlasting Father, Prince of Peace,"** and (Micah 5:2) **"But you Bethlehem Ephrathah though you are small among the clans of Judah, out of you will come for me one who will be ruler over Israel, whose origins are from of old from ancient times."**

Keep in mind that these prophetic scriptures were written hundreds of years before the birth of Jesus in Bethlehem. Now look at this; the same prophet Isaiah later on made this prophesy about the crucifixion death of the same Messiah whose birth both he and the prophet Micah had predicted. Here is an excerpt from his prophesy about the death of Jesus Christ – The Messiah: Isaiah 53: 1-12: **"He is despised and rejected of men; a man of sorrows, and acquainted with grief: and we hid as it were our faces from him; he was despised, and we esteemed him not. Surely he hath borne our griefs, and carried our sorrows: yet we did esteem him stricken, smitten of God, and afflicted. But he was wounded for our transgressions, he was bruised for our iniquities: the chastisement of our peace was upon him; and with his stripes we are healed. All we like sheep have gone astray; we have turned every one to his own way; and the LORD hath laid on him the iniquity of us all. He was oppressed, and he was afflicted, yet he opened not his mouth: he is brought as a lamb to the slaughter, and as a sheep before her shearers is dumb, so he openeth not his mouth. He was taken from prison and from judgment: and who shall declare his generation? for he was cut off out of the land of the living: for the transgression of my people was he stricken. And he made his grave with the wicked, and with the rich in his death; because he had done no violence, neither was any deceit in his mouth. Yet it pleased the LORD to bruise him; he hath put him to grief: when thou shalt make his**

soul an offering for sin, he shall see his seed, he shall prolong his days, and the pleasure of the LORD shall prosper in his hand."

There are clear and indisputable prophesies regarding the miraculous birth and sacrificial death of the Lord Jesus. They include a range of events from his birth at Bethlehem to his death, burial and resurrection at Jerusalem. Now let's take a look at some highlights of this Messiah – Jesus Christ within the range and scope of his life between Bethlehem and Jerusalem. Who is this Jesus?

The question – Who is this Jesus? was not a casual or trivial question in the minds and in the conversations of people in the land of Israel. These were people whose religious life was interwoven with their secular life. They looked to their Rabbis or spiritual leaders for answers when they had questions about events and people past and present.

When this baby was born in Bethlehem and it was reported that an infant was born whose parents were of the lineage of Abraham the renowned patriarch and father of the Jewish nation – The Rabbis were not impressed! Why not you ask? You would think that when they heard from credible sources that angels announced his birth to shepherds and that the angels gave the shepherds specific directions to find the infant Jesus in exactly the same town where the Old Testament prophet Micah predicted that this Messiah – child would be born, that they would think it over. You would also think that when they heard that astrologers – kings followed a star of curious origin to the exact location where Jesus was born, that these Rabbis would sit up and think that this could just may be the Messiah prophesied in Old Testament scripture who would be a descendant of Abraham.

Did you ever hear the saying: "A man convinced against his will is of the same opinion still?" That's a good fit for the religious leaders of that period. By the way they were referred to repeatedly in the Gospels as Pharisees and Sadducees. For about three (3) decades after the buzz triggered this unusual infant's birth, there was little news about his growing up except that he lived in Nazareth with his family. Nazareth was not a place of residence that attracted the adoring attention of any self-respecting Israelite as they were called then. The Israelis,—Jews as we refer to them today—were comfortable with the news blackout on Jesus. They did not have to keep bringing up his name at their synagogues or at the temple since even his name was so controversial. By this time, the news got around that an angel appeared to Joseph (a descendant of David) in a dream and told him to be assured that his virgin wife would miraculously bear a son and that she should name him Jesus, because he shall save his people from their sins. This was just the start of religious tumult, confusion and contention in the land of Israel. Then suddenly, after three (3) decades of silence on the subject of Jesus, this controversial figure appeared walking unaccompanied on the Jordan River bank. Believe me, when I first read these words from the Gospel of John I could understand why the presence of Jesus alone, without his words or his works of miracles, caused so much fuss and furor in the religious community. Here are the words that came from the mouth of a wilderness prophet named John the Baptist when he first saw Jesus: (John 1:29) **"Behold the lamb of God that takes away the sin of the World."**

From here on the saga of Jesus builds and builds, and kept building. Every increment of the life of Jesus on planet earth was a display of God's plan in reaching out to have an endearing personal relationship with people like you and me. That is so profound and literally so breathtaking, that we need to catch our breath for a second or two. Then we should ask ourselves so what are we thinking about Jesus?

CHAPTER 24

LET'S THINK ABOUT JESUS

What do you think?

So, Jesus has now emerged out of over two decades of obscurity and is publicly identified as the Lamb of God who is to take away the sin of the world. The person who makes this excited announcement is a seeming eccentric but respected Jewish prophet. In today's lingo looking at his outfit, you may think of him as a kind of hobo. This man John who they call the Baptist had some disciples some of whom later followed Jesus soon after his debut on the bank of the Jordan River.

This Messiah who John-the-Baptist announced to be far greater that he could ever be would quickly become the most controversial figure in Jewish history. A few things to keep in mind so we can keep Jesus in proper perspective. First, the Jewish people ever since they took possession of the land that was promised to Abraham and his off-springs, they have been repeatedly harassed, attacked, captured and victimized. These serial events endured by the Jewish people would guarantee the abolition of a nation of people, if God did not make those promises to Abraham, especially the one we discussed earlier directly related to Jesus who Matthew in his genealogy described as the son of Abraham. Speaking of military assaults on their nation, the mighty Romans did not spare releasing their might against the tiny nation of Israel. The Romans overran Israel and set up a version of Roman rule that mercifully allowed the Jews to practice their religion without Roman interference.

Listen carefully to this reason for the fierce controversy that characterized the public appearance of Jesus. As you can see from the history of mankind, no human being wants to be enslaved or dominated by another. There is a deep seated and burning desire in the human spirit to be free! You can see that surging desire for freedom played in the recent series of revolts against dictators (Arab spring) in the Middle Eastern Muslim States even as we are speaking. The Jews in the time of Jesus, looked eagerly for the promised Messiah, and now here was their big question! "Was this Jesus the long awaited Messiah?" Was He really? This was the heart, core, and center of Jewish Religious controversy. The long awaited Messiah was expected to champion their cause and free them from the political yoke of the mighty Roman Empire. How did this square with their expectations of the Messiah that John-the-Baptist proclaimed he was and that Jesus himself repeatedly claimed to be.

I think it's fair to mention that while I am far from being an expert in matters of Jewish Religious history, I have more than a personal passing interest in the person of Christ. That's why I can sketch for you some snippets of His life and mission without even looking at the written information in the Bible we have been reading from as we travel.

By the way, the main source of information about the life and work of Jesus is scripted in the four (4) Gospels of the New Testament: Matthew, Mark, Luke and John. There are historical commentaries and corroborations found in "The Antiquities of the Jews" by a Jewish historian names Josephus. The four (4) Gospels are the first books of the New Testaments. Not sure if you are familiar with their content. If you are not, join the club. Sometime ago I had no literary interest in this kind of reading either. All four reporters on the activities of Jesus mention that people who saw Him and heard Him speak were amazed at His presence and astounded at His words. Should be interesting to hear and think about some of **HIS WORDS**.

CHAPTER 25

LET'S THINK ABOUT
THE WORDS OF JESUS

No man spoke as He did

There are no records of history found anywhere showing that this man Jesus received any kind of formal or informal education. Fact is, if we believe He was who He claimed to be –The Son of God and God the Son – He would be the founder and originator of all knowledge and would need no teacher or tutor. This God claim by Jesus triggered bitter controversy and put him on a collision course with the powerful religious leaders.

Regarding the words of Jesus, everyone or most people who heard him speak, even his detractors, remarked with astonishment that they never heard anyone speak like this man. So, it seemed that his words distinguished him and made him an instant celebrity speech maker. Ironically there were those who considered this charismatic speechmaker a troublemaker! When you think of the circumstances and the content of his words, they were not difficult to listen to or difficult to understand. For example: The Gospel authors starting with Matthew, reports that Jesus started preaching, saying: **"Repent! For the kingdom of Heaven is at hand."** Then he started recruiting disciples, by just saying **"come follow me."** Later He took his disciples by the side of a mountain and delivered the immortal **"Sermon on the mount."** In this sermon there was no theological mombojumbo, just plain compassionate gestures and concepts about people and God, and about people living kindly, graciously and thoughtfully among themselves.

The Gospel written by Mark jumps right into the story of Jesus by telling us that during His first public appearance His first words were simple and straight forward: **"Come follow me and I will make you fishers of men."** These were His words to some fishermen who were awestruck by His presence. The Gospel written by Luke (a Physician) presents Jesus appearing in public at his hometown synagogue in Nazareth. At this religious service, He was invited to read from a chapter of the Old Testament prophesy of Isaiah. At the end of the verse in the text that referred to Him as the Messiah, "He said that this day is the scripture fulfilled in your ears." Luke records that all who heard Him wondered at the gracious words that came from His mouth.

The last of the four Gospels authors presents Jesus in His first public appearances in pretty much the same venues and situations. John reports Jesus actively recruiting some disciples by responding to their questions: "Master, where do you live? What does He reply? **"Come and see."** From our very brief excerpts on the words of Jesus in the early stages of His public life we can say there was nothing exceptional about **the words He spoke.**

Why was there these awestruck expressions by those who heard His words: **"Never a man spoke like this man. He speaks with authority and not as do the religious leaders."** Can you think of a reason for these gushing compliments? Are you saying you can't, at the moment? Well, let me offer a thought. I think that although His words were clear and plain and in no way exceptional, the person Jesus who spoke those words was and is exceptional! He had to be to command that kind of mystique. To clarify any fuzzy thinking about His words – he at one time said that – **"The words that I speak unto you they are spirit and they are life."** Now that is heavy material. We will pick that up later.

We have not yet scratched the surface of the **Words of Jesus,** but it looks like we are moving closer toward the end of our **Thinking Wonderland** adventure, so let's switch to thinking about some of the **Works of Jesus.** You know, I was just thinking at the mention of the works of Jesus we are about to discuss, and the exceptional attributes he displayed, that only a God-man could complete the works he announced that he came to do. Remember the great masters of music and art? If you recall from your art appreciation courses – they all left unfinished works! Beethoven, Brahms, Mozart, even Michelangelo the legendary painter and sculptor, left paintings unfinished and sculpting incomplete. We will find that this exceptional person who claimed to be a revelation of God, and was one with God, is God the Son and the Son of God. We will also find that He not only did amazing, astounding, awe-inspiring works but He finished all the work that he came to do. So, here we go to think about some of His works.

CHAPTER 26

LET'S THINK ABOUT
THE WORKS OF JESUS

His work was to execute God's Plan
for a personal relationship with man

If you think about it, work is a wonderful invention. It presents all kinds of challenges and presents all kinds of opportunities. Do you like to work or do you like work itself? I like both. Some people say thank God it's Friday. I say thank God it's Monday, so I can start working again. When I was growing up I couldn't wait to start working so I could earn money to do things I wanted to do. There was another thing about work that I thought about and that was the kind of work I wanted to do. One of the reasons I was so fascinated with young children is that they are so imaginative. I had a lot of imaginations about work. I saw people doing very hard work and got very little pay or respect. I saw my mom working like a Trojan Horse to take care of me and I admired her creativity and her courage to tackle anything no matter how difficult. No work, she said, was degrading! I did not think or agree with that at all. I saw some work that people were doing and admired their skill or brain power. On the other hand

I saw some work that was just not my cup of tea. Do you know that you imitate people you admire without even knowing it. I admired pilots who flew planes and landed them safely. I admired engineers who designed complex things and solved problems that relieved people from the distress of demanding rigors of manual work. I saw that the work of engineers could be found in every crevice of human existence. My admiration for the work of medical care givers has never faded. I have always had trouble comparing the medical people's work with that of the engineer and scientists. Can you detect my bias?

That aside, although work that brings sweat to the brow of the laborer is the result of man's expulsion from paradise, because of his disobedience, work is still the key cornerstone of our civilization. So I believe what the Bible says: That God sent His Son into the world replete with sin, sadness and suffering so that He would start and finish **a unique work.** The Bible says that God sent His Son Jesus into a world in universal moral condition described as gross darkness.

Jesus upon arrival publicly announced that He had come to work on this project. The project was a challenge that only Jesus (Messiah) could handle. It included the work of preaching the good news to the poor, healing the sick and brokenhearted, deliverance to captives, recovering sight to the blind, and setting at liberty those that were bound. The grand finale of His work – TO BE THE SAVIOR OF ALL MANKIND.

It would be a huge and unfortunate digression if we didn't keep in mind that this work project that Jesus announced, was planned by God to reach out to man for a personal relationship. The Gospels tell story after story of the works of Jesus during about three (3) years of His public time on earth. While I am talking with you, I am reflecting on the amazing works of Jesus. His works ran the gamut from a miracle of chemistry (turning water into wine) to enhance a happy event to a miracle of recovery in an impossible situation where sorrow and sadness prevailed. The first was at a wedding and later at the grave of Lazarus.

If we have no other reason to think that marriage between a man and a woman is favored by God, then look at Jesus at the wedding at Cana, a small town in Galilee. John, the Gospel reporter, says that Jesus showed up with His disciples at the wedding. As the wedding celebration progressed the wine regressed until all the wine disappeared. Then we are told Jesus came to the rescue, and simply asked that they fill some water pots with pure water. Then with no hocus-pocus – just the power and presence of this man who claimed to be the Son of God, there was wine enough to keep the celebration going!

Have you thought of the first miracle of Jesus? Have you wondered why he chose this first miracle to start the series of his works? By the time we are finished this spellbinding conversation we will be asking all kinds of thinking questions. Here is my thought about the wedding event: It seems that marriage is God's plan for human reproduction. You will recall from our visit to the book of genesis, God created Adam and Eve and clearly stated that the essential reason for their creation was to procreate or multiply – producing human species like themselves.

He told them the intent of their spousal relationship was that they should be as one and live as one. Their children should, at some point, leave the custody of their parents and cleave to each other. Where are you going with this, are you asking? Well, it seems that Jesus was, through this miracle, teaching this lesson: Sometimes, early in a marriage, there will exist situations that can intercept happiness, but when Jesus is present a solution is assured. The works of Jesus as reported in the Gospels were unending. Day after day He was working to address some situation of need, usually the needs were severe and beyond the reach of ordinary human capacity.

I just mentioned that day after day Jesus kept working. That's what the Gospels report. Before we get to some examples of His day-after-day work and some specifics on His workdays, it occurred to me that although work was invented to meet human needs, a rest period was also ordered so that we may recharge our batteries. For the Jews, this rest period: the Sabbath. Today we call this rest period: the eagerly anticipated <u>WEEKEND!</u> Isn't it interesting how one thought leads to another? Let me share with you an incident that connects with the thoughts about working day-after-day without a break day. I pulled up to a fuel service station and asked for a "fill-up" and noticed the price had sprinted up again compared to my last "fill-up". I started a small talk conversation with this mild-mannered, polite and very courteous gentleman who was on duty alone at the pump. Our conversation led to my question about his work schedule. He told me, quite amazingly, that he worked over eighty (80) hours per week. I said when do you get some time off – a rest day? His reply – never! I work every day – the boss likes it and I like it. I like it because, I keep a little to take care of my expenses and I send the rest home to Pakistan where my family lives. They cannot come here so I must support them from here with the money I earn. I work every day – no overtime pay! I am tired, but it's good. I take care of my family. By this time, he had filled my tank with golden fuel (over $4.00 per gal.) and I exchanged a few words about the Koran (which he was surprised that I read) and I told him to cheer up and try reading the Bible (which I promised to bring to him next time).

As I drove away, I was deeply touched. Here was a poor humble man pushing himself to human limits to meet what he considered to be a moral obligation to his family in Pakistan. I thought of him working every day no break, day after day, and saying to a perfect stranger – It's good – I like, I send much money to my family – I happy! Incidentally, I will be back to visit him. I was deeply touched and prayed for him as I drove away.

The casual conversation I had with this Pakistani gentleman at the fuel service station made me think of Jesus and his work schedule. The Gospels show him in early morning prayer, perhaps followed by a breakfast meeting with His twelve (12) disciples before starting a day stretching from dawn to dusk. It seems he kept this schedule every day of the week including the Sabbath when He took some time to visit a synagogue. We know this because repeatedly he was accused by religious leaders, of illegal activity on the Sabbath. Sick people crossed His path on the Sabbath-day and He healed them. There was one occasion when a woman with a chronic condition that made her a cripple for eighteen (18) years living without hope for recovery or relief.

Hear this! Jesus saw her and called out to her, and said **Woman, you are loosed from that crippling condition!** Then he laid His hands on her; and immediately she was healed – and she praised God big time! This by the way, was done on a Sabbath-day. As you might expect, this got the attention of the chief Rabbi, who immediately reminded the people, who witnessed this amazing work of healing that this was a clear violation of Sabbath rules. He added, that there are six (6) days available for all kinds of work including healing, so the Sabbath must never be breached. Jesus responded by referring to times when they did things on the Sabbath day that they considered to be urgent necessity and of course understandably very convenient.

Jesus further stated, in emphasizing His work and mission, **"I**

must work while it is day, the night cometh when no man can work." Jesus also on another occasion said (paraphrase) "the sunlight gives us twelve (12) working hours and then the darkness falls and we stumble in the dark because the light has disappeared for a while." The work that Jesus assigned himself to do and to finish took him to and through all the known and unknown areas of the Holy Land. Speaking of Holy Land, this was the land that God promised to Abraham and his descendants – for the Jews of that period it was the PROMISED LAND. Now, before the eyes of all (not only Jews) this land had become – The Holy Land! This was because the Holy Son of God had arrived with an agenda that started at Bethlehem and would appear to end in Jerusalem.

On His way to Jerusalem, Jesus continued working day-after-day, starting with early morning prayer and ending the day in prayer. At one time when he was ready to prepare some of His disciples to become apostles (missionaries) He carefully selected twelve (12) of those he had personally called to follow Him. Just before He advised them of the intensive program of information and instruction they would experience, he spent all night in Prayer. I think this was to teach His disciples the priority and importance of prayer especially at a crucial time and at a critical juncture in their development. Speaking of the juncture we have reached in thinking about the works of Jesus – the half has not been told! The words of John, the author of the fourth Gospel, are these: **"there are so many other things (works) that Jesus did, if they were all recorded the world itself could not contain the books that should be written."** A touch of hyperbole, by John, but we get the point concerning the works of this exceptional and charismatic person Jesus the Messiah!

CHAPTER 27

LET'S THINK ABOUT
THE WONDER OF JESUS

They wondered at the mighty power of God

The Gospel writer, Luke, gives us a series of insights into the Wonder of Jesus. Wonder, in the sense that <u>His presence</u> was so kind and gentle, yet unquestionably authoritative: <u>His compassion</u> moved Him to tears as He wept over the beloved city of Jerusalem and at the grave of Lazarus, who he later raised from the dead. <u>His healing powers</u> that allowed Him to heal all the disease of sick people. The record says – He healed them all. He was the miracle physician who hung no stethoscope around his neck and did not have or need a prescription pad. He did not even have to diagnose any disease. No physical condition could resist his healing power. Then there was His astounding ability to take five (5) loaves and two (2) fish and inflate a young boy's lunch to become a full course meal for over five thousand people, and we are told there were leftovers that could feed many more.

At about this point, Luke records that all the people who saw these spectacular events were **all amazed at the mighty power of God.**

But while they wondered at all these things that Jesus did, He said to them: Listen carefully, I am about to head for Jerusalem where I will be crucified. These disciples were understandably confused because you would think that for all the amazement and wonder expressed about the miraculous works He performed, He would be headed to Jerusalem for a city-wide celebration in recognition of His words, works, and the wonder that He evoked where ever he went.

The fact is that the master plan for God's personal relationship with man required that Jesus should go to Jerusalem and be crucified there and be resurrected from there and ascend to heaven from there, and some unexpected day return to gather from all nations of people those who expressed faith in Him as personal Savior and consequently experience a personal relationship with God through Him. Remember those <u>Promises, Promises, Promises,</u> we discussed earlier, that God gave to Abraham? You remember the last one that we called <u>the ultimate promise:</u> It said that through the descendants of Abraham would all the nations of the earth be blessed. Remember also that we read in the very first verse of the New Testament that Jesus was a direct descendant of Abraham and that He was announced, by an angel, to be called Jesus (Savior) because He would save His people from their sins? Later on we hear Jesus Himself saying: **"For God so loved the world that He gave His only begotten Son that whosoever believeth in Him should not perish but have eternal life." WHAT A STORY! WHAT A STORY! WHAT A STORY!**

Our conversation has not come even realistically close to scratching the surface of an **Omnipotent, Omniscient, Omnipresent God** reaching out to sinful mortals, with <u>the good news of His Grace, Love and Mercy.</u> Why is that? Is that your final question? My best answer? Another question, what are you thinking my answer should be? Simply this! It's the theme that caught our attention as we are near the end of our stroll through **Thinking Wonderland i.e.,** that it is possible for anyone to have a personal relationship with God. Got a pen handy? Jot down these three (3) scriptures and I will mention them again before we say goodbye.

1. John chapter 3, verse 16

2. Romans chapter 10, verse 9

3. Romans chapter 10, verse 13

CHAPTER 28

BEFORE WE SAY GOODBYE

Think of what we have been thinking!

This has been a really exciting adventure for me! What say you? Are you saying that for you it has been equally exciting? Then we have just become charter members of the same club where Stimulating Thinking is the top item on the agenda. Stimulating Thinking! We especially enjoyed discursive discussions about such a wide variety of topics. We also covered a lot of miles strolling through this "imaginary" **Thinking Wonderland.** I almost captioned this final part of our dialogue: One, Two, Three Propinquity! I thought of that rarely used word, Propinquity, first, because of its poetic flavor but also because we have become so closely connected during our wonderland stroll just thinking and talking back and forth day after day.

During my senior year in Engineering school at the City College of New York, I was assigned a research paper on Theoretical Physics that led to my reading of George Gamow's classic work titled: "One, Two, Three, Infinity." In the introduction of his book he tells the story of an underdeveloped region in Southwestern Africa where the inhabitants were not able to count to any more than the number three (3). They count everything – men, women, children, cattle, days, months, years – everything ends at three (3). Their number system restricted their counting to one, two, three and the rest was infinity or what we may consider endless. Time has gone by so swiftly, and we can certainly count to more than three (3), but coincidentally we chose to cover three (3) main topics of thinking. **One** was: **"What Are You Thinking About God;"** Two was: **"What Are You Thinking About Man vs. Man"** and Three was: **"What Are You Thinking About God Having A Personal Relationship With Man (Is That Possible)"**.

Before we say goodbye, a quick and brief recap of three (3) main topics of our thinking may be useful and even refreshing. In the first section on "What are You Thinking About God" we noticed that Jesus and Socrates were early models of Teachers who prompted their students to **Think.** There we picked up on the inspired observation in the Bible book of Job that stated: **There is a Spirit in man and the inspiration of the Almighty gives him understanding** (Job 32:8). We recalled that a legendary icon like King David of Israel, thought about God as he gazed into the mysterious constellations of stars, the sun, moon and the awesome heavenly bodies, he could only say: **"When I think of the heavens and the greatness of God, why does He even think of us mortals."**

Then we spent some time at the "steps of logical thought" and discovered that the Bible was and is the source of all information about God and this mysterious universe of ours. After some rambling thinking and discussing about famous scientists and how they thought about God, we also went on to think quite extensively using illustrations from the Bible, about the three (3) main attributes of God – His **O**mnipotence, His **O**mniscience and His **O**mnipresence.

After a couple of rest breaks we resumed our stroll through **Thinking Wonderland** by kicking off the second topic: **What Are You Thinking About Man vs. Man.** This was a real challenge, first to put the topic in rational perspective and then to think through the network of contradictions in the nature of man. If you recall, the core of our thinking back and forth was about man's puzzling duality. One poet, Edwin Markham, as he contemplated this mystery of man wrote: **"Is this the thing the Lord God made and gave to have dominion over sea and land; to trace the stars and search the heavens for power; to feel the passion of eternity?"**

I could sense your emotions as perhaps you did mine, especially as we made some real life references to people who displayed such contrary behavior. It was this duality in man that got us stumped! As always, we can count on "inspired" poets to come to our rescue when we become ensnared by the cobweb of our philosophies. By the way, do you recall we discussed the fact that we are all philosophers? In the sense that, as life throws us curve balls, we try to think our way through so many things that seem sometimes to make no sense at all. That is our claim to be certified philosophers!

Fortunately, for our conversation, our choice was to think about the <u>Good</u> part of man's <u>Duality</u> first. Our illustrative examples of Mother Teresa, Albert Schweitzer, David Livingstone, Hudson Taylor and so many, many others, made it worthwhile for us to explore some of their memorable good deeds toward their fellowmen with no desire, intent, or expectation for any material reward! That was heartwarming and made us wish that there were more people like those in the world today. Then reluctantly, we turned to the bad side of man if only to face the reality of our topic i.e., man is characterized by a strange duality. Another poet came to our rescue regarding the baffling nature of man. If you

remember the lines from Sam Walton Foss' poem: The House by
the Side of the Road."

> *I see from my house by the side of the road,*
> *By the side of the highway of life,*
> *The men who press with the ardor of hope,*
> *The men who are faint with the strife.*
> *But I turn not away from their smiles nor their*
> *tears*
> *Both parts of an infinite plan;*
> *Let me live in my house by the side of the road*
> *And be a friend to man.*

I sometimes recall the lines from another bard who put these
words in the mouth of Mark Anthony as he gave the Eulogy
at Caesar's funeral – he said: **"The evil that men do lives after
them but the good is often interred with their bones."** How
true! But let us not forget to thank God, that by His providential
plan, there are more good people in our world than there are
bad people. Now, a few reflections on the bad people. We will
not allow their <u>evil deeds</u> to live after them – not in our brief
conversation about them. So we will be brief.

So for people like Adolf Hitler and Joseph Stalin and others of
their ilk we have concluded that these are people who like those
in our illustrations of Cain and Abel, of Bible record; Abel on the
one hand made the choice to please God with his offering while
on the other hand Cain chose a selfwilled path that led him to
murder his own brother.

This conundrum in human nature we traced back to Genesis, the
Bible book of beginnings. There we discovered as expected, the
origin of this duality in man. Whereas he was created pure and
innocent and given specific instructions from his creator, he chose

the route of disobedience, by eating of the forbidden tree of good and evil. This "original" mishap by Adam and Eve, regrettably, unfortunately and tragically molded all of us members of the human race into this puzzling duality of our behavior toward our fellow human beings.

We then discussed God's provision to restore the broken relationship which occurred as a result of our ancestors' flagrant disobedience. Our third and final section at this point, we launched into the "meat and potatoes" of our thinking wrap-up i.e., God's plan to have a personal relationship with man – on His terms: God in His infinite wisdom, further back that we can think before the formation of the world, developed a plan to rescue and restore mankind – the progeny of Adam and Eve – to a total relationship with himself.

This plan would allow these errant human beings, (our fellow mortals) all of whom inherited the gene pool of our forebears, to become regenerated or born again, i.e., experience a new life on earth and the certain hope of eternal life. This is God's glorious plan that brings us full circle. Three hundred and sixty degrees. Started in Paradise and back to Paradise! What is that plan that would enable man to love and serve God with all his/her heart, with all his/her mind, with all his/her soul? My very dear friend, let me tell you with all my heart, with all my mind, with all my soul: **It is God's magnificent plan of Salvation!**

Do you recall that I asked you to jot down three (3) verses of scripture? Perhaps you forgot. Not to worry! The first one fits squarely into answering the question: what is that God's magnificent plan you referred to a moment ago? You do remember that a short time ago after our last rest break we started a stream of thoughts about Jesus? About Jesus Himself, about His words, about His works and about His wonder. Now let's pick up on a verse from the New Testament words that will clearly explain the magnificent salvation plan. The first verse you jotted down was: John 3:16 which says: **"For God so loved the world that He gave His only begotten Son that whosoever believes in Him should not perish but have everlasting life."**

For such a complex arrangement to turn errant sinful persons (which we all are) into born-again children of God, is very heavy theology and not at all the intent of our friendly conversation. So let me go now to the other two (2) verses you jotted down earlier. In Romans 10:9: the verse says (notice its focus on Jesus) **"That if you will confess with your mouth the Lord Jesus and believe in your heart that God raised Him from the dead, you will be saved."** In other words, you can receive God's magnificent salvation. Then the last of the three (3) verses you jotted down: Romans 10:13. Now, you see this next verse – Romans 10:13 that we are looking at together, every time I read it or refer to it, I have an emotional connection with a life-changing experience of many years ago.

This verse 13 says: **"If you shall call on the Name of the Lord Jesus you shall be saved."** To be honest I did not understand the theology of that verse, but I'll tell you this – I sincerely and wholeheartedly believed what it said! It said as I translated it, that If I believed verse 9, (not mentally but in and from my heart) earlier read, verse 13, would land me squarely in **God's magnificent salvation plan.** It said, I would be saved. This means I would experience a new life on this earth. This means that this salvation plan would guarantee my <u>personal relationship</u> with God regardless of trials, tribulations, adversities, distresses, disappointments, you name it. None of these things would separate me from the magnetic love of God and His endearing grace.

These were historic moments for me! I resonated with President

Bush's response who when asked a few years ago to explain his statement about being a born-again Christian – said: "don't know much theology, but all I know is that I accepted Christ by faith and HE CHANGED MY LIFE!

These my friend are passionate moments for me as we are about to say goodbye. They are passionate because I know that the Lord Jesus, who I accepted by the way of those New Testament scriptures verses I quoted, has not only changed but made a miracle of my life. He has taken me from the poorest of the poor and elevated me to literally sit among the princes in corporate America and abroad, and in many areas of distinction in academia. Most importantly – my highest achievement is to be His humble servant.

Perhaps we can lighten up our pre-farewell conversation by a little imaginary exercise. Try to imagine you are listening to your favorite musical rendition! You go first and then I will say the lyrics of a favorite score of mine rendered by a favorite gospel choir of mine – no, it's not the Mormon Tabernacle Choir or the Brooklyn Tabernacle Choir – it's the Galilee Gospel Chapel Singers! Never heard of them? Let me say the words of one of my favorite pieces that they sing so beautifully and I hope these words connect with your thinking: Here it goes:

> *To God be the glory, great things He hath done, '*
> *So loved He the world that He gave us His Son,*
> *Who yielded His life an atonement for sin,*
> *And opened the life gate that all may go in.*
> *Oh come to the Savior make no delay for*
> *Here in his word he has shown us the way.*

How did you like the words of the beautiful song about Jesus and about God and the Holy Spirit? Wasn't that beautiful even without the orchestra? If you really think about those words you will notice how seamlessly they fit into the frame of our thinking about God's magnificent salvation plan. That plan is detailed in the greatest story ever told! The story of God (unimaginable); the story of man (unbelievable); the story of God's relationship to man and man's personal relationship to God (unfathomable). The key to the door of God's magnificent salvation plan – The Lord Jesus Christ who the musical score just intoned: "Oh come to the Savior make no delay for here in his word he has shown us the way."

Sincerely, my friend I express to you my deepest gratitude for the opportunity to have the pleasure of your company in taking this trip with me through **Thinking Wonderland.** When we started I said, we had promises to keep and miles to go before we sleep. I think we kept our promises; we have completed our imaginary miles of travel and can now go off to get some sleep. When you wake up what will you be doing? Thinking! Thinking! Thinking! Then what? You answer that! One last thing, then we do a high five or hand shake. I promised you a brief insight into the basis of my thinking about God – remember? It's briefed in the Epilogue!

So again, my friend **before we say goodbye,** may I have your permission to say a silent prayer that by God's grace **our thinking will not be in vain.** And now we can high five or shake hands, as you wish! Reluctantly, my friend – **so long! Farewell! Adios! au revoir! das vidaniya! Sayonara! Andio! Shalom! Ajo! Arrivederci! Auf Wiedersehen**

EPILOGUE

There is nothing like an event whose time has come. It seems clear from all my recent and current circumstances that the time had come for me to open up the door of my heart and mind for some written sharing of my thinking, not about me, but about **my Lord and my God.**

He deserves all the praise and adoration that I am not capable of ascribing. For quite some time I pondered how to reach the widest possible audience with an engaging conversation about Thinking! Specifically, Thinking about an amazing God who dwells in such glorious and sacred light that no man can approach, but in love, mercy and grace has arranged to embrace everyone (personally) who approaches Him through His Son – The Lord Jesus Christ. In a brief series of conversations I tried to start and keep the theme of our thoughts focused on the topics of Thinking as we (you and I) made this excursion through a fictitious **Thinking Wonderland.** Thanks for making the trek with me!

My apologies again to those of you, who over the years, kept insisting that I write a book reflecting my incredible experiences in various adventures over several decades. I feel a sense of relief in sharing, through this book, a virtual conversation with an audience including people I met in the many careers that I have been privileged to pursue. Equally of interest in the audience are so many of my readers whom I have never met in person. I became increasingly aware that, although I was never ashamed of my faith or hesitant to give God all the praise He deserves in "church circles," I did not have the best record of personally witnessing to others especially as I moved up the corporate ladder and later as a successful entrepreneur. In other words – I missed many opportunities, outside church circles, that should have been embraced.

Regrettably, I have been visited by the uncomfortable guilt of not using more direct contact in social opportunities when I could – that is having a conversation about – **What Are You Thinking?** This book has been a partial redemption for me.

In my closing comments would you really like to hear what I am Thinking? I sincerely think that no stroke of the most learned pen can write, or no words of the most eloquent tongue can tell of the wonder and glory of this **O**mnipotent, **O**mniscient, **O**mnipresent God who generously blesses us and mercifully forgives us when we fail, and loves us everlastingly even when we are not always loveable.

Sometimes in my feeble attempt to emote about God, I shout – He is absolutely fantastic! David of Bible times took a crack at expressing similar emotions in one of his Psalms by saying: "God is very great!" My words: "God is beyond very great!" That's exactly why I wrote this book! Currently, my experience is one of adjusting to life without my beloved late wife, Phyllis. I never thought that any kind of adjustment could ever get me through this rigorous passage of grief. I loved her as my own soul. The God of all comfort has not failed one word of His promise.

My ongoing discovery of this magnificent God is one of ongoing amazement. He meets us at the point of our deepest needs.

A God who took a poor boy from the miry clay of poverty and set his feet on the granite rock of faith and kept him, by His grace while guiding him through the many adventurous decades of his life, including rising to the executive level in the world's largest corporation, is **WORTHY TO BE PRAISED!!!** What do you think? Well that's the God I tried to get you thinking about! I know not why God's wondrous love to me He has made known, or why unworthy of such love He bought me for his own. But I know who I believe and am persuaded that he is able to keep that which I have committed unto Him against that day. GLORIA DIO!

GOD BLESS!

CONTACT THE AUTHOR

Nothing would be more pleasing than to hear from my "virtual" travelling companions who spent time with me in **Thinking Wonderland.**

I am honored to be currently serving in a pastoring ministry at Bible-centered Galilee Gospel Chapel in Queens, New York. I am also honored to serve as visiting professor at my alma mater at the City College of New York School of Engineering. So I am not really completely retired. Seems I am as busy as ever. Despite my activities you can be sure I'll be delighted to hear from you. Why? Just to hear what you are Thinking!

Reach me at:

E-mail BGPCCNY@GMAIL.COM

APPENDIX I

Excerpts From Our Conversation
In Thinking Wonderland

- Thinking by the human mind is uniquely given to us by God
- Thinking is the ancestor of all our actions – good and bad
- The awesome mysteries of our universe make us think
- Thinking springs from the words we learn growing up. From words we form thoughts and raise questions
- The thinking geniuses of science are the result of God's revealing to them His secrets of nature
- Thinking about a personal relationship with God results from God-inspired craving in the heart of everyone
- The Holy Bible has the answers to all questions and is the source of all information and instructions for our guide in this life and the next

APPENDIX 2

1. Thought you may like to use the note space below to jot down what you are Thinking after reflections on our stroll through **Thinking Wonderland**

2. Briefly note what action, if any, you plan to take regarding a personal relationship with God

If you need a free copy of a Bible or a pocket New Testament, please see the page titled: Contact the Author